Python Projects for Beginners

Create Games, Tools, and Apps
While Learning Code the Fun Way

Booker Blunt

Rafael Sanders

Miguel Farmer

Boozman Richard

How to Scan a Barcode to Get a Repository

1. **Install a QR/Barcode Scanner** – Ensure you have a barcode or QR code scanner app installed on your smartphone or use a built-in scanner in **GitHub, GitLab, or Bitbucket.**

2. **Open the Scanner** – Launch the scanner app and grant necessary camera permissions.

3. **Scan the Barcode** – Align the barcode within the scanning frame. The scanner will automatically detect and process it.

4. **Follow the Link** – The scanned result will display a **URL to the repository.** Tap the link to open it in your web browser or Git client.

5. **Clone the Repository** – Use **Git clone** with the provided URL to download the repository to your local machine.

Chapter 1: Introduction to Python and Setting Up Your Development Environment

Overview: Why Python is Perfect for Beginners

Python is one of the most versatile and beginner-friendly programming languages available today. Whether you're just starting with coding or looking to expand your programming skills, Python offers a seamless learning curve, making it ideal for both novices and seasoned developers. It's a high-level, interpreted language that emphasizes simplicity and readability, which is why it has become the go-to choice for those looking to learn coding quickly and effectively.

Python's philosophy revolves around simplicity and minimalism. The syntax is clean and intuitive, which makes it easier to focus on problem-solving rather than getting bogged down by complex language rules. In fact, Python code often reads like English, making it much more accessible to beginners.

But why exactly is Python a great choice for newcomers?

1. **Clear, Readable Syntax**: Python is designed to be easy to read and write. You don't have to worry about complicated punctuation or memorizing overly complex rules. The structure is straightforward, and even if you make mistakes, Python's error messages are clear, helping you understand and fix your issues quickly.

2. **Powerful Libraries and Frameworks**: Python has a rich ecosystem of libraries and frameworks that allow you to do everything from building websites and automating tasks to data analysis, machine learning, and game development. You'll find Python in use in industries like healthcare, finance, and robotics, which means that learning Python opens up a world of professional opportunities.

3. **Wide Community Support**: Python has an active and thriving global community, which means that you'll never be short of resources when learning. You can easily find tutorials, forums, and free libraries that can help you solve any problem you encounter. This community-driven approach makes it easy to get help, find solutions, and improve your skills.

4. **Cross-Platform Compatibility**: Whether you're using Windows, macOS, or Linux, Python is compatible across all these platforms, making it flexible and easy to run your Python code in different environments.

By the end of this chapter, you'll not only have Python installed and set up on your machine but also be ready to start writing Python scripts, building your coding confidence one step at a time.

Topics: Installing Python, Setting Up IDEs (VSCode, PyCharm), and Understanding Basic Syntax

Before diving into writing Python code, we first need to set up the development environment. This is where we configure our machine with the necessary tools to write, test, and run our Python scripts.

1. Installing Python

To begin programming with Python, we first need to install the Python interpreter on your machine. Python runs on virtually any operating system (Windows, macOS, Linux), so no matter what system you're using, you'll be able to get started.

Installation Steps for Windows:

1. Go to the official Python website: https://www.python.org/downloads/
2. Click on the download link for the latest stable version of Python. Make sure you download the version compatible with your operating system (usually the latest version).
3. Run the installer. During installation, make sure to check the box that says "Add Python to PATH." This ensures that Python can be accessed from the command line.
4. Once installed, open the Command Prompt (CMD) and type `python --version` to verify that Python has been successfully installed.

Installation Steps for macOS:

1. macOS comes with Python 2.x pre-installed, but we need the latest version of Python (3.x). The easiest way to install it is using the Homebrew package manager.

2. Open the Terminal and type `brew install python3` to install the latest version of Python 3.

3. Once installed, you can check the version by typing `python3 --version` in the Terminal.

Installation Steps for Linux (Ubuntu/Debian-based systems):

1. Open your terminal and type `sudo apt update` to ensure your package list is up to date.

2. To install Python 3, type `sudo apt install python3`.

3. Once installed, you can check the version by typing `python3 --version`.

Why Is It Important to Install Python Properly?

Having Python correctly installed is crucial for running your Python scripts smoothly. When Python is added to your system's PATH, it allows you to run Python directly from the command line or terminal, which is an essential step for writing and executing Python programs.

2. Setting Up Your IDE: VSCode and PyCharm

While you can technically write Python code in any text editor, a specialized Integrated Development Environment (IDE) makes coding far more efficient by providing features like syntax highlighting, auto-completion, debugging tools, and more.

Two of the most popular Python IDEs are **Visual Studio Code (VSCode)** and **PyCharm**. Let's explore both so you can choose the one that works best for you.

Installing VSCode:

1. Go to the official Visual Studio Code website: https://code.visualstudio.com/
2. Download the version compatible with your operating system.
3. Install VSCode, and once installed, launch the application.
4. To start writing Python code, you'll need to install the Python extension for VSCode. You can do this by clicking on the Extensions icon in the sidebar (the square icon on the left) and searching for "Python." Click "Install" on the Python extension provided by Microsoft.

Why VSCode?

VSCode is lightweight, highly customizable, and works well for Python development. It offers IntelliSense (auto-completion), integrated Git support, and a terminal for running your Python code directly within the editor.

Installing PyCharm:

1. Go to the official PyCharm website:
   https://www.jetbrains.com/pycharm/download/
2. Download the free version (Community) or the paid version (Professional) depending on your preference.
3. After installation, open PyCharm, and you'll be prompted to configure your Python interpreter, which you can link to the Python version you installed earlier.

Why PyCharm?

PyCharm is an all-in-one Python IDE that's specifically tailored for Python development. It provides advanced features like a code inspector, a visual debugger, and integrated unit testing. For beginners, it offers an incredibly supportive environment with useful tutorials and a hands-on interface for tackling larger projects.

3. Understanding Basic Python Syntax

Now that we have our development environment set up, it's time to dive into Python's syntax—the set of rules that define how we write Python code.

Variables and Data Types:

Python is a dynamically typed language, which means that you don't need to declare the type of a variable when you create it. The interpreter automatically assigns the type based on the value you assign to the variable.

```python
# Declaring variables in Python
name = "Alice"  # String
age = 25  # Integer
height = 5.6  # Float
is_student = True  # Boolean
```

Indentation in Python:

Unlike many programming languages that use braces ({ }) to define blocks of code, Python uses indentation to separate code blocks. This is one of the reasons why Python code is so clean and readable.

For example:

```python
if age >= 18:
    print("You are an adult.")
else:
```

```
print("You are a minor.")
```

Notice that the lines inside the `if` and `else` blocks are indented. This indentation is crucial in Python and is how the interpreter knows which statements belong to which block of code.

Hands-on Project: Creating Your First Python Script – "Hello, World!"

It's time to get our hands dirty and write our first Python script! "Hello, World!" is the classic first program for any programming language, and Python is no exception.

Here's how you can write your first script:

1. Open your IDE (VSCode or PyCharm).
2. Create a new file and save it as `hello_world.py` (make sure the extension is `.py`, which stands for Python).
3. In the file, type the following code:

```python

# This is a comment. Comments are not executed by
Python.
# They are helpful for explaining your code to
others.
```

```
print("Hello, World!")
```

4. Save the file and run it. You should see `Hello, World!` printed in your console or terminal.

Explanation:

- `print()` is a built-in Python function that outputs text to the screen.
- `"Hello, World!"` is a string, which is text enclosed in quotation marks.

Takeaways: How to Navigate Through the Python Development Environment

By the end of this chapter, you should have a clear understanding of the Python development environment and how to use it effectively.

Here's a recap of the key points covered:

- **Installing Python**: You now know how to install Python on different operating systems and check the version to verify the installation.

- **Setting Up Your IDE**: You've learned how to install and configure both VSCode and PyCharm, two of the most popular Python IDEs.
- **Basic Syntax**: You now understand the fundamentals of Python's syntax, including how to declare variables, work with data types, and use indentation to define code blocks.

With these basics in place, you're ready to start writing Python programs and exploring the countless possibilities that Python offers. As you continue learning, the Python environment will become your go-to workspace for building everything from simple scripts to complex applications.

Chapter 2: Variables, Data Types, and Operators

Overview: Understanding Variables, Data Types, and Operators

In any programming language, including Python, understanding how to store and manipulate data is fundamental. This chapter introduces some of the core concepts of programming: **variables**, **data types**, and **operators**. These are the building blocks of any program, and mastering them will help you handle different kinds of data in your code.

- **Variables**: Think of a variable as a container or storage space in your program where you can store data that might change during the execution of your program. For instance, you might store a user's name, age, or a score in a game in variables.
- **Data Types**: These define the type of value a variable can hold. Python offers several built-in data types, such as strings, integers, floats, and booleans.
- **Operators**: Operators are symbols that allow you to perform operations on variables and values. There are several types

of operators, including **arithmetic operators, comparison operators**, and **logical operators**, each serving different purposes.

By the end of this chapter, you will not only understand how to work with numbers, text, and boolean logic but also be able to perform calculations and manipulate data effectively.

Topics: Working with Numbers, Text, and Boolean Logic

1. Variables: Storing and Referencing Data

Variables are essential in programming as they allow you to store and reference data in your program. Think of a variable as a "box" where you can place a value, and then refer to it by its name throughout your code.

In Python, creating a variable is simple. You don't need to declare the type of the variable ahead of time. Python is **dynamically typed**, which means the type of the variable is automatically determined based on the value assigned to it.

Example:

```python
python
```

```python
name = "Alice"     # String (text)
age = 25           # Integer (whole number)
height = 5.7       # Float (decimal number)
is_student = True  # Boolean (True or False)
```

- **String**: A sequence of characters, enclosed in either single quotes (') or double quotes (").
- **Integer**: A whole number without any decimal part.
- **Float**: A number that has a decimal point.
- **Boolean**: A type that can either be True or False.

Once a variable is created, you can reference it anywhere in your program. For example:

```python
python
```

```python
print(name)   # Outputs: Alice
print(age)    # Outputs: 25
```

2. Data Types: Understanding the Building Blocks

In Python, the **data type** determines what kind of data a variable can store and how that data behaves. Let's explore the common data types in Python:

Strings (`str`):

Strings are used to represent text in Python. You can store any sequence of characters inside single or double quotes. Here's how you declare a string:

```python
message = "Hello, Python!"
```

Integers (`int`):

Integers represent whole numbers. Python handles large numbers gracefully, without worrying about overflow.

```python
age = 30
```

Floats (`float`):

Floats are numbers with a decimal point. They are used when you need to represent fractions or numbers with greater precision.

```python
temperature = 36.5
```

Booleans (`bool`):

Booleans are used for logic and control flow. A boolean variable can either be `True` or `False`.

```python
is_raining = False
```

Lists (`list`):

A list is a collection of ordered items. Lists can store items of different data types (numbers, strings, etc.). You define a list using square brackets.

```python
colors = ["red", "blue", "green"]
```

Dictionaries (`dict`):

Dictionaries are collections of key-value pairs. They allow you to store data in a way that pairs a key with a specific value.

```python
person = {
    "name": "Alice",
    "age": 30,
    "city": "New York"
}
```

Each data type in Python has specific operations that can be performed on it. For example, you can concatenate strings, perform arithmetic on numbers, or check the length of a list.

3. Operators: Manipulating Data

Operators in Python are symbols that help us perform operations on variables and values. There are three primary types of operators we'll cover in this chapter: **arithmetic operators**, **comparison operators**, and **logical operators**.

Arithmetic Operators

Arithmetic operators are used to perform mathematical operations on numbers (integers and floats). Here are the most common arithmetic operators:

- + (Addition): Adds two numbers together.
- – (Subtraction): Subtracts one number from another.
- * (Multiplication): Multiplies two numbers.
- / (Division): Divides one number by another and returns a float.
- / / (Floor Division): Divides one number by another and returns the integer quotient (rounded down).
- % (Modulus): Returns the remainder of a division operation.
- ** (Exponentiation): Raises one number to the power of another.

Example:

```python
python

x = 10
y = 3

# Addition
print(x + y)   # Output: 13

# Subtraction
print(x - y)   # Output: 7

# Multiplication
print(x * y)   # Output: 30

# Division
print(x / y)   # Output: 3.3333...

# Floor Division
print(x // y)   # Output: 3

# Modulus
print(x % y)   # Output: 1

# Exponentiation
print(x ** y)   # Output: 1000
```

Comparison Operators

Comparison operators are used to compare two values. These operators return a boolean value (`True` or `False`) depending on the comparison.

- `==` (Equal to): Checks if two values are equal.
- `!=` (Not equal to): Checks if two values are not equal.
- `>` (Greater than): Checks if the left value is greater than the right value.
- `<` (Less than): Checks if the left value is less than the right value.
- `>=` (Greater than or equal to): Checks if the left value is greater than or equal to the right value.
- `<=` (Less than or equal to): Checks if the left value is less than or equal to the right value.

Example:

python

```
x = 10
y = 5

print(x == y)   # Output: False
print(x != y)   # Output: True
print(x > y)    # Output: True
```

```
print(x < y)     # Output: False
print(x >= y)    # Output: True
print(x <= y)    # Output: False
```

Logical Operators

Logical operators are used to combine conditional statements and return a boolean value. They are essential when you need to check multiple conditions.

- and: Returns `True` if both conditions are true.
- or: Returns `True` if at least one condition is true.
- not: Reverses the boolean value of a condition.

Example:

python

```
x = 10
y = 5

# AND operator
print(x > 5 and y < 10)   # Output: True

# OR operator
print(x > 15 or y < 10)   # Output: True

# NOT operator
print(not (x > 5))   # Output: False
```

Hands-On Project: Build a Simple Calculator that Performs Basic Arithmetic Operations

Now that we've covered the theory behind variables, data types, and operators, it's time to put this knowledge into action. Let's build a simple calculator that can perform basic arithmetic operations—addition, subtraction, multiplication, and division.

Step-by-Step Instructions for Building the Calculator

1. **Plan the Calculator:**
   o We need to build a program that can take two numbers and an arithmetic operator (+, -, *, /).
   o The program should perform the operation and return the result.

2. **Set Up the Code:**

python

```python
# Step 1: Define the function that will perform the
calculation
def calculator(num1, num2, operator):
    if operator == "+":
        return num1 + num2
    elif operator == "-":
        return num1 - num2
    elif operator == "*":
        return num1 * num2
    elif operator == "/":
        if num2 != 0:
            return num1 / num2
        else:
            return "Error: Division by zero"
    else:
        return "Invalid operator"
```

```
# Step 2: Get user input
num1 = float(input("Enter the first number: "))
num2 = float(input("Enter the second number: "))
operator = input("Enter the operator (+, -, *, /): ")

# Step 3: Call the calculator function and print the
result
result = calculator(num1, num2, operator)
print(f"The result is: {result}")
```

3. **Explanation of the Code:**

   o **Function Definition**: The `calculator` function takes in two numbers (`num1` and `num2`) and an operator as arguments. It then performs the appropriate operation based on the operator provided.

   o **Input Handling**: We use `input()` to get the user's numbers and the operator. Since `input()` returns a string, we use `float()` to convert the user input into numerical values.

   o **Error Handling**: The division operation includes an error check to handle the case where the user tries to divide by zero.

   o **Result Output**: Finally, the program prints out the result of the operation.

Step 4: Test the Calculator

Run the program, and try entering different values to test each operation:

1. Input: 5, 3, +

   o **Output:** The result is: 8.0

2. Input: 10, 2, /

   o **Output:** The result is: 5.0

3. Input: 15, 0, /

   o **Output:** Error: Division by zero

Takeaways: How to Perform Basic Calculations and Handle User Input

By the end of this chapter, you should have a strong understanding of how to:

1. **Work with Variables**: Store and manipulate different types of data (numbers, text, booleans).

2. **Use Data Types**: Recognize and use different data types such as integers, floats, and strings effectively in your code.

3. **Apply Operators**: Use arithmetic operators for performing calculations, comparison operators for decision-making, and logical operators for combining conditions.

4. **Handle User Input**: Collect user input via the `input()` function and perform calculations based on that input.

This chapter gives you the building blocks necessary for more complex programs. Understanding how to use variables, data types, and operators will empower you to write more advanced applications and solve problems programmatically.

Chapter 3: Control Flow: Conditionals and Loops

Overview: Learn How to Use Decision-Making Structures and Repetition in Python

In any program, there are times when you need to make decisions or repeat certain actions multiple times. This is where **control flow** comes in. Control flow allows your program to make decisions based on conditions and repeat actions when necessary. These capabilities are fundamental to building interactive and functional programs.

This chapter will introduce you to Python's **decision-making structures** and **loops**, two essential concepts that will allow you to write more dynamic and interactive code.

- **Conditionals** allow you to perform different actions based on whether a condition is `True` or `False`.
- **Loops** help you repeat actions until a specific condition is met, avoiding the need to write repetitive code.

By mastering these tools, you will have more control over how your program behaves, which is crucial for solving real-world problems and creating more efficient code.

Topics: if, else, elif Statements, and for, while Loops

1. Conditionals: Making Decisions in Python

A **conditional statement** enables you to make decisions in your code. The most commonly used conditional statements in Python are if, else, and elif (short for "else if").

These statements allow your program to test conditions and decide which path to take based on whether those conditions are True or False.

1.1 if Statement

The if statement allows you to execute a block of code only if a specific condition is True.

Syntax:

```python

if condition:
    # Code to execute if the condition is True
```

Example:

```python

age = 20

if age >= 18:
    print("You are an adult.")
```

In this example, the condition age >= 18 is checked. If the condition is True, the program prints "You are an adult."

1.2 else Statement

The else statement is used when you want to specify an action to take when the if condition is False. The block of code inside the else block will execute if the condition in the if statement is False.

Syntax:

```python

if condition:
    # Code to execute if the condition is True
```

```
else:
    # Code to execute if the condition is False
```

Example:

python

```
age = 16

if age >= 18:
    print("You are an adult.")
else:
    print("You are a minor.")
```

In this example, since age is 16, the else block will execute, and the program will print "You are a minor."

1.3 elif Statement

The elif statement is used when you have multiple conditions to check. It's short for "else if" and allows you to check additional conditions if the previous ones were False.

Syntax:

python

```
if condition1:
    # Code to execute if condition1 is True
```

```
elif condition2:
    # Code to execute if condition2 is True
else:
    # Code to execute if all conditions are False
```

Example:

```python
python

age = 25

if age < 18:
    print("You are a minor.")
elif age < 21:
    print("You are a young adult.")
else:
    print("You are an adult.")
```

Here, the program checks if the `age` is less than 18 first, then if it's less than 21. If neither condition is met, the program will default to the `else` block.

---

2. Loops: Repeating Actions

Sometimes, you need to repeat a specific action multiple times without writing the same code over and over. Loops are essential for such scenarios. Python provides two primary types of loops: the **for loop** and the **while loop**.

2.1 for Loop

A `for` loop allows you to iterate over a sequence of elements, such as a list, tuple, string, or range of numbers. It's perfect for situations where you want to perform an action a specific number of times or iterate through a collection.

Syntax:

```python

for item in sequence:
    # Code to execute for each item in the sequence
```

Example:

```python

colors = ["red", "blue", "green"]

for color in colors:
    print(color)
```

This loop will print each color in the list `colors`, one by one.

You can also use the `range()` function with a `for` loop to repeat an action a certain number of times.

Example:

python

```
for i in range(5):
    print(f"This is iteration {i + 1}")
```

Here, the `for` loop will run five times, printing a message for each iteration.

2.2 while Loop

The `while` loop is used when you want to repeat an action **as long as a condition remains True.** Unlike the `for` loop, which is typically used when you know how many times you want to repeat something, the `while` loop continues until a specific condition is no longer true.

Syntax:

python

```
while condition:
    # Code to execute as long as the condition is
True
```

Example:

```python
count = 0

while count < 5:
    print(f"Count is {count}")
    count += 1  # Increment the counter
```

In this example, the loop will continue to print the value of count until it reaches 5. Each time, the count is incremented by 1.

Hands-On Project: Build a Guessing Game Where the User Guesses a Number and Gets Feedback

Let's now put what we've learned into practice. We will create a **guessing game** where the user has to guess a randomly selected number within a specific range.

Step 1: Plan the Game

- The computer will pick a random number between 1 and 100.
- The user will try to guess the number.

- After each guess, the program will give feedback: whether the guess was too low, too high, or correct.
- The game will keep running until the user guesses the correct number.

Step 2: Code the Game

python

```python
import random

# Step 1: Generate a random number
number_to_guess = random.randint(1, 100)

# Step 2: Initialize the user's guess
guess = None

# Step 3: Give the user instructions
print("Welcome to the Guessing Game!")
print("I'm thinking of a number between 1 and 100.
Try to guess it!")

# Step 4: Start the loop
while guess != number_to_guess:
    # Step 4.1: Get the user's guess
    guess = int(input("Enter your guess: "))

    # Step 4.2: Provide feedback based on the guess
    if guess < number_to_guess:
```

```
    print("Too low! Try again.")
  elif guess > number_to_guess:
    print("Too high! Try again.")
  else:
    print(f"Congratulations! You guessed the
number {number_to_guess} correctly!")
```

Step 3: Explanation of the Code

1. **Importing the random module:** The `random.randint(1, 100)` function generates a random integer between 1 and 100. This is the number the user has to guess.

2. **Setting up the guessing loop:**
   o   We use a `while` loop, which continues until the user guesses the correct number.
   o   Inside the loop, we prompt the user for their guess with `input()`, then convert it to an integer using `int()`.
   o   Depending on whether the guess is lower, higher, or equal to the number to guess, we provide feedback.

3. **Exiting the loop**: Once the user guesses the correct number, the `while` loop ends, and the program prints a congratulatory message.

Step 4: Try it Yourself

Now, you can try the game and test different inputs to ensure the feedback is correct. If you want to challenge yourself further, you can modify the game to limit the number of guesses allowed or add hints for the user based on their previous guesses.

Takeaways: How to Control the Flow of Your Code Based on Conditions

By the end of this chapter, you should be comfortable with:

1. **Making Decisions Using Conditionals**: You can now use `if`, `elif`, and `else` statements to make decisions in your code. These tools allow you to test conditions and direct your program to take different actions depending on the result of those tests.

2. **Repeating Actions with Loops**: You've learned how to use both `for` and `while` loops to repeat actions in your code. Loops allow you to handle repetitive tasks efficiently, whether it's iterating through a collection or repeating an action until a specific condition is met.

3. **Building Interactive Programs**: Through the guessing game project, you now know how to create interactive programs

that respond to user input. You've also learned how to use loops and conditionals together to create engaging, dynamic applications.

With these tools, you'll be able to write more complex programs that can interact with users, make decisions, and repeat tasks efficiently. As you continue learning, you'll explore how to combine control flow with other Python features to create even more powerful programs.

Chapter 4: Functions: Creating Reusable Code

Overview: Understanding the Importance of Functions in Programming for Reusability

In programming, one of the most important principles is to **avoid repetition**. As your code grows, having redundant or repetitive code can make it difficult to maintain, debug, and extend. Functions allow you to **organize** your code into reusable blocks that can be invoked as needed. By doing so, you reduce repetition and increase the clarity of your code.

This chapter focuses on the concept of **functions** in Python and explains how to define, use, and return values from functions. Functions are fundamental to writing clean, efficient, and maintainable code. By breaking your program into smaller, manageable chunks of functionality, you make your code easier to test, debug, and modify.

At the end of this chapter, you will understand how to:

- **Define functions** that perform specific tasks.

- **Pass parameters** to functions, allowing you to provide inputs that influence the function's behavior.
- **Return values** from functions, enabling the function to output results that can be used elsewhere in the program.
- **Organize your code** into reusable blocks to make it more readable and maintainable.

By leveraging functions, you'll learn how to break down complex problems into smaller, more manageable parts, allowing you to tackle each part individually and logically.

Topics: Defining Functions, Passing Parameters, Returning Values

1. Defining Functions in Python

A **function** is a named block of code designed to perform a specific task. Once a function is defined, you can call it multiple times throughout your program without needing to rewrite the same code over and over.

Why Use Functions?

- **Avoid Redundancy**: Functions help reduce repetitive code. Instead of writing the same logic multiple times, you can define it once and reuse it as needed.
- **Improve Readability**: Functions break down a large program into smaller, understandable blocks of code, making the program easier to follow.
- **Enhance Reusability**: Functions are reusable. Once written, you can call them whenever necessary, passing different arguments and getting results.

1.1 Basic Syntax for Defining Functions

In Python, functions are defined using the `def` keyword, followed by the function name and parentheses containing any parameters (optional). The body of the function is indented beneath the definition.

Syntax:

```python
def function_name(parameters):
    # Code to execute
    return value  # Optional
```

- `def`: The keyword that tells Python you're defining a function.

- `function_name`: The name of the function, which should follow standard naming conventions (usually lowercase, words separated by underscores).
- `parameters`: Optional input values that the function uses when executed. If no input is required, you leave the parentheses empty.
- `return`: Optional statement that sends a result back to where the function was called.

Example:

python

```
def greet():
    print("Hello, world!")
```

This is a simple function named `greet` that prints "Hello, world!" when called. Notice that it doesn't take any parameters and doesn't return any value.

1.2 Calling Functions

Once a function is defined, you can call it using its name followed by parentheses.

Example:

```python
```

```python
greet()   # Calls the function, printing "Hello,
world!"
```

Functions can be called multiple times throughout your code, making them reusable.

2. Passing Parameters to Functions

While the basic function example above is simple and doesn't accept any input, most functions require **parameters**. Parameters allow you to pass values into the function that can affect its behavior.

When defining a function, you specify the **parameters** inside the parentheses. These parameters act as placeholders for the values you will provide when calling the function. These values are known as **arguments**.

Syntax:

```python
```

```python
def function_name(parameter1, parameter2):
    # Code to execute
```

```
    return result
```

Example:

```
python
```

```python
def greet(name):
    print(f"Hello, {name}!")
```

Here, `name` is a parameter that allows us to pass in a specific value when calling the function.

Calling the function with arguments:

```
python
```

```python
greet("Alice")   # Output: Hello, Alice!
greet("Bob")     # Output: Hello, Bob!
```

By passing different arguments to the `greet()` function, you can reuse the same function to greet different people.

3. Returning Values from Functions

A function can **return** a value, which means it gives an output that can be used elsewhere in your program. The `return` statement sends the result of the function back to the point where it was called.

Once a function reaches a `return` statement, it exits, and no further code within the function is executed.

Syntax:

python

```
def function_name(parameter1, parameter2):
    result = parameter1 + parameter2
    return result
```

Example:

python

```
def add_numbers(a, b):
    return a + b

sum = add_numbers(5, 3)    # sum will store the result
of 5 + 3, which is 8
print(sum)    # Output: 8
```

In this example, the `add_numbers()` function returns the sum of two numbers. The result is stored in the variable `sum`, and then printed.

4. Functions with Multiple Parameters and Return Values

Functions can accept multiple parameters, and you can also have functions that return more than one value. In Python, you can return multiple values from a function by separating them with commas. These values are returned as a **tuple**.

Example:

python

```
def get_user_info(name, age):
    return name, age

user_info = get_user_info("Alice", 30)
print(user_info)   # Output: ('Alice', 30)
```

Here, the function returns both name and age as a tuple, which can be unpacked when calling the function.

Hands-On Project: Create a Function that Calculates the Area of Different Shapes (Circle, Square, Rectangle)

Now that we've covered the basics of defining functions, passing parameters, and returning values, let's apply this knowledge in a hands-on project. We will create a function that calculates the area of different shapes (circle, square, and rectangle) based on user input.

Step 1: Plan the Project

1. We will define a function that calculates the area of:
    - **Circle:** Area = π * radius^2
    - **Square:** Area = side^2
    - **Rectangle:** Area = length * width
2. The function will prompt the user for the shape they want to calculate the area for and then ask for the necessary dimensions (e.g., radius, side length, or width).
3. The function will calculate the area and return it.

Step 2: Write the Code

python

```python
import math

def calculate_area(shape):
    if shape == "circle":
        radius = float(input("Enter the radius of the circle: "))
        area = math.pi * (radius ** 2)
        return area
    elif shape == "square":
        side = float(input("Enter the side length of the square: "))
        area = side ** 2
        return area
```

```python
    elif shape == "rectangle":
        length = float(input("Enter the length of the
rectangle: "))
        width = float(input("Enter the width of the
rectangle: "))
        area = length * width
        return area
    else:
        return "Invalid shape"

# Get the user's choice of shape
shape = input("Enter the shape (circle, square,
rectangle): ").lower()

# Call the function and display the result
area = calculate_area(shape)
print(f"The area of the {shape} is: {area}")
```

Step 3: Explanation of the Code

1. **Function Definition:**
   o The calculate_area() function takes one
     parameter shape, which determines which shape the
     user is calculating the area for.
2. **Conditional Logic:**
   o Inside the function, we use an if-elif-else
     statement to check the type of shape and calculate
     the area accordingly.

o For each shape, the function prompts the user for the necessary dimensions (radius, side length, or length and width) and calculates the area using the appropriate formula.

3. **Returning the Area:**

o The area is returned to the point where the function was called, and we print the result.

Step 4: Testing the Function

1. **Input:** "`circle`" and radius 5

o **Output:** `The area of the circle is: 78.53981633974483`

2. **Input:** "`square`" and side length 4

o **Output:** `The area of the square is: 16.0`

3. **Input:** "`rectangle`" with length 6 and width 3

o **Output:** `The area of the rectangle is: 18.0`

Step 5: Enhancing the Function

You can enhance this function by:

- Adding error handling to ensure the user provides valid numeric input.
- Allowing the user to calculate the area of more shapes in the future by adding more conditions in the function.

- Creating additional functions to calculate other properties (perimeter, volume, etc.).

Takeaways: How to Organize Your Code into Functions for Better Readability and Reusability

By the end of this chapter, you should be comfortable with:

1. **Defining Functions**: You now know how to define functions in Python, enabling you to organize your code into reusable blocks that are easy to understand and maintain.
2. **Passing Parameters**: Functions allow you to pass in data that can influence the function's behavior, making your code more flexible and interactive.
3. **Returning Values**: You can use the `return` statement to send a result from a function to where it is called, allowing your programs to work with the outputs of functions.
4. **Improving Readability and Reusability**: Functions enable you to avoid repeating code, make your programs more readable, and reduce the risk of errors.

Functions are fundamental to structuring your code efficiently. They allow you to break down large problems into smaller, more manageable parts. By mastering functions, you'll be able to write cleaner, more modular, and maintainable Python code.

This chapter has set the foundation for working with functions. In future chapters, we will build on this knowledge to tackle more advanced concepts like **scope**, **lambda functions**, and **recursion**, which will further enhance your ability to write powerful Python programs.

Chapter 5: Lists, Tuples, and Dictionaries: Storing and Organizing Data

Overview: Learn How to Use Data Structures to Organize Data Efficiently

When building applications in Python, you'll need to store and organize data. This is where **data structures** come into play. Data structures are essential tools that allow you to manage, store, and manipulate data in a way that's both efficient and easy to work with. In Python, some of the most commonly used data structures are **lists, tuples**, and **dictionaries**.

- **Lists**: These are ordered collections of items, which can be changed after their creation. Lists are flexible and commonly used to store multiple items.
- **Tuples**: Similar to lists, but immutable. Once created, tuples cannot be modified.

- **Dictionaries**: These are collections of key-value pairs. They allow you to store data in a way that is highly efficient for searching and retrieval.

In this chapter, we will dive deep into these three data structures. You will learn how to access, modify, and iterate through data efficiently. We'll also walk through a hands-on project where you'll build a **contact book** that allows you to add, update, and search for contacts using these data structures.

By the end of this chapter, you'll have a solid understanding of how to use lists, tuples, and dictionaries to manage and organize data in Python.

Topics: Lists, Tuples, and Dictionaries – Accessing, Modifying, and Iterating Through Data

1. Lists: Organizing Data with Ordered Collections

A **list** is one of the most versatile and commonly used data structures in Python. A list is an ordered collection of items, which means the order in which you add items to a list is maintained. Lists are **mutable**, meaning you can change, add, or remove items after the list has been created.

1.1 Defining Lists

You can define a list in Python using square brackets `[]`. Items inside a list are separated by commas.

Syntax:

```python
my_list = [item1, item2, item3]
```

Example:

```python
fruits = ["apple", "banana", "cherry"]
```

In this example, `fruits` is a list containing three string elements.

1.2 Accessing List Items

You can access individual elements in a list by referring to their index, with the first element having an index of 0.

Example:

```python
fruits = ["apple", "banana", "cherry"]
```

```
print(fruits[0])    # Output: apple
```

To access the last item in the list, you can use a negative index.

Example:

```
python
```

```
print(fruits[-1])    # Output: cherry
```

1.3 Modifying List Items

Since lists are mutable, you can change the value of an item by using its index.

Example:

```
python
```

```
fruits[1] = "orange"
print(fruits)    # Output: ['apple', 'orange',
'cherry']
```

1.4 Adding and Removing Items

You can add new elements to a list using the `append()` method, or insert them at a specific position with `insert()`. You can remove items using `remove()` or `pop()`.

Examples:

python

```
fruits.append("grape")   # Adds 'grape' at the end
fruits.insert(1, "kiwi")   # Inserts 'kiwi' at index 1
fruits.remove("apple")   # Removes 'apple'
popped_item = fruits.pop()   # Removes the last item
and returns it
```

1.5 Iterating Through Lists

To iterate over the elements of a list, you can use a `for` loop.

Example:

python

```
for fruit in fruits:
    print(fruit)
```

This will print each item in the `fruits` list.

---

2. Tuples: Storing Data That Doesn't Change

A **tuple** is similar to a list in that it can store a collection of items. However, unlike lists, tuples are **immutable**, meaning their contents cannot be changed once they are created.

2.1 Defining Tuples

You define a tuple using parentheses `()`.

Syntax:

```python
my_tuple = (item1, item2, item3)
```

Example:

```python
coordinates = (10, 20, 30)
```

In this example, `coordinates` is a tuple containing three integer elements.

2.2 Accessing Tuple Items

You can access elements in a tuple in the same way as in a list, using an index.

Example:

```python
print(coordinates[0])   # Output: 10
```

2.3 Iterating Through Tuples

You can iterate over a tuple using a `for` loop, just like you would with a list.

Example:

```python
python

for coordinate in coordinates:
    print(coordinate)
```

2.4 Why Use Tuples?

Tuples are used when you want to store data that should not be modified after creation. They are faster than lists in terms of iteration and memory usage, so they can be beneficial when you have a large set of data that doesn't need modification.

---

3. Dictionaries: Storing Data with Key-Value Pairs

A **dictionary** is a data structure that stores **key-value pairs**. This means that each item in the dictionary has a unique key, and the value is the data associated with that key.

3.1 Defining Dictionaries

You define a dictionary using curly braces {}. Each key is separated from its value by a colon, and each pair is separated by a comma.

Syntax:

```python
my_dict = {key1: value1, key2: value2, key3: value3}
```

Example:

```python
contact_info = {"name": "Alice", "age": 25, "city": "New York"}
```

In this example, `contact_info` is a dictionary containing three key-value pairs: `"name"` maps to `"Alice"`, `"age"` maps to `25`, and `"city"` maps to `"New York"`.

3.2 Accessing Dictionary Items

You can access a dictionary item by referencing its key.

Example:

```python
```

```python
print(contact_info["name"])   # Output: Alice
```

3.3 Modifying Dictionary Items

Since dictionaries are mutable, you can modify the value associated with a key by simply assigning a new value.

Example:

python

```python
contact_info["age"] = 26
print(contact_info)   # Output: {'name': 'Alice',
'age': 26, 'city': 'New York'}
```

3.4 Adding and Removing Items

To add new key-value pairs to a dictionary, you simply assign a value to a new key. To remove an item, you can use the `del` statement.

Examples:

python

```python
contact_info["phone"] = "123-456-7890"  # Adds a new
key-value pair
del contact_info["city"]  # Removes the "city" key-
value pair
```

You can iterate over the keys, values, or key-value pairs of a dictionary using a `for` loop.

Examples:

python

```
for key in contact_info:
    print(key)  # Prints the keys

for key, value in contact_info.items():
    print(f"{key}: {value}")  # Prints both keys and values
```

Hands-On Project: Build a Contact Book Where the User Can Add, Update, and Search for Contacts

Now that we've explored the basics of lists, tuples, and dictionaries, let's apply this knowledge to a hands-on project: building a **contact book**.

In this project, the user will be able to:

1. Add new contacts.

2. Update existing contacts.

3. Search for contacts by name.

We'll use a **dictionary** to store each contact's details, where the contact's name will be the key and the contact details (such as phone number and email) will be the value.

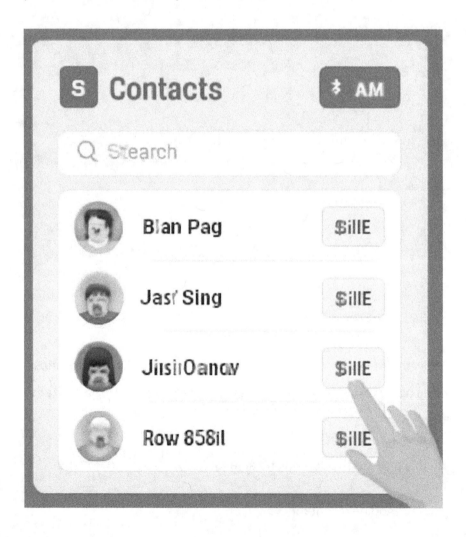

Step 1: Plan the Project

The contact book will have the following features:

- **Add a contact**: Users can input a name, phone number, and email to add a new contact.
- **Update a contact**: Users can update the contact's phone number or email.
- **Search for a contact**: Users can search for a contact by name and view their details.
- **Exit the program**: Users can exit the program at any time.

Step 2: Write the Code

python

```python
def add_contact(contact_book):
    name = input("Enter the name of the contact: ")
    phone = input("Enter the phone number: ")
    email = input("Enter the email address: ")
    contact_book[name] = {"phone": phone, "email":
email}
    print(f"Contact for {name} added successfully!")

def update_contact(contact_book):
    name = input("Enter the name of the contact to
update: ")
    if name in contact_book:
```

```python
        phone = input(f"Enter new phone number for
{name}: ")
        email = input(f"Enter new email address for
{name}: ")
        contact_book[name] = {"phone": phone,
"email": email}
        print(f"Contact for {name} updated
successfully!")
    else:
        print(f"Contact for {name} not found.")


def search_contact(contact_book):
    name = input("Enter the name of the contact to
search for: ")
    if name in contact_book:
        print(f"Contact Details for {name}:")
        print(f"Phone:
{contact_book[name]['phone']}")
        print(f"Email:
{contact_book[name]['email']}")
    else:
        print(f"Contact for {name} not found.")


def main():
    contact_book = {}
    while True:
        print("\nContact Book Menu:")
        print("1. Add Contact")
        print("2. Update Contact")
```

```
print("3. Search Contact")
print("4. Exit")
choice = input("Choose an option: ")

if choice == "1":
    add_contact(contact_book)
elif choice == "2":
    update_contact(contact_book)
elif choice == "3":
    search_contact(contact_book)
elif choice == "4":
    print("Exiting the Contact Book.")
    break
else:
    print("Invalid choice. Please try
again.")

# Run the program
main()
```

Step 3: Explanation of the Code

1. **Add a Contact:** The add_contact() function prompts the user for contact information and stores it in the dictionary.

2. **Update a Contact:** The update_contact() function allows the user to modify an existing contact's details.

3. **Search for a Contact:** The search_contact() function searches for a contact by name and displays their details.

4. **Main Program Loop**: The `main()` function drives the program, showing a menu to the user and executing the corresponding functions based on their choice.

Step 4: Testing the Contact Book

Run the program and test all features:

1. Add new contacts.
2. Update existing contacts.
3. Search for contacts.
4. Exit the program.

Takeaways: Understanding How to Work with Complex Data Structures

By the end of this chapter, you should have a solid understanding of:

1. **Lists**: How to use lists to store and manipulate ordered collections of data. You've learned how to access, modify, add, remove, and iterate through list items.
2. **Tuples**: How to use tuples for storing data that should not be modified. Tuples are a great option when you want an immutable collection of data.

3. **Dictionaries**: How to use dictionaries for storing key-value pairs, allowing you to efficiently access, update, and manage data. Dictionaries are particularly useful for cases where data needs to be referenced by a unique key.

4. **Hands-on Experience**: Through the contact book project, you've learned how to apply these data structures to solve a real-world problem. You now understand how to build programs that store, update, and search data efficiently using Python.

These three data structures—lists, tuples, and dictionaries—are foundational to working with data in Python. By mastering them, you'll be able to handle more complex data management tasks and write more efficient, readable code.

Chapter 6: File Handling: Reading from and Writing to Files

Overview: How to Work with Files in Python – Reading and Writing

In programming, data is often stored in files for persistent storage. This allows your program to save data and retrieve it even after the program has ended or the computer has been turned off. In Python, **file handling** is an essential skill that enables you to read from and write to files on your system.

File handling allows your Python programs to interact with external data, whether that data is text, numbers, or even binary data. By using file handling, you can create programs that save user preferences, log data, load previously saved information, or manipulate files such as text documents or CSV files.

In this chapter, we will explore the various ways you can work with files in Python, including:

- **Opening files** to access them for reading or writing.
- **Reading from files** to extract and use stored data.
- **Writing to files** to store data persistently.
- **File modes**, which determine how files are accessed (read, write, append, etc.).

By the end of this chapter, you will understand how to manage files in Python, whether you're saving data, logging events, or reading data for analysis.

Topics: Opening Files, Reading and Writing Data, File Modes

1. Opening Files in Python

Before you can read from or write to a file in Python, you need to **open** it. Python provides a built-in `open()` function to access files. This function returns a **file object** that can be used to interact with the file.

Syntax:

```python

file_object = open('filename', 'mode')
```

- `'filename'`: The name of the file you want to open. This can be a file path if the file is located in a different directory.
- `'mode'`: The mode in which to open the file (e.g., read, write, append).

There are several **modes** available when opening a file:

- `'r'`: **Read mode** – Opens the file for reading. The file must exist.
- `'w'`: **Write mode** – Opens the file for writing. If the file does not exist, it will be created. If the file exists, it will be overwritten.
- `'a'`: **Append mode** – Opens the file for appending data at the end of the file. If the file does not exist, it will be created.
- `'b'`: **Binary mode** – Used in combination with other modes for binary files (e.g., `'rb'` for reading a binary file).
- `'x'`: **Exclusive creation** – Opens the file for writing, but the file must not exist. If the file exists, an error will be raised.

Example:

python

```python
# Open a file in read mode
file = open('data.txt', 'r')
```

In this example, `data.txt` is opened for reading. If the file doesn't exist, Python will raise an error.

2. Reading from Files

Once a file is opened in read mode, you can use various methods to read the data inside the file.

2.1 Reading the Entire File

The `read()` method allows you to read the entire contents of the file at once.

Example:

```python
file = open('data.txt', 'r')
content = file.read()
print(content)
file.close()
```

This will print all the contents of `data.txt`.

2.2 Reading Line by Line

You can also read a file line by line using the `readline()` method. This is useful for processing large files without loading everything into memory at once.

Example:

```python
python
```

```python
file = open('data.txt', 'r')
line = file.readline()
while line:
    print(line, end='')  # 'end' prevents an extra
newline from being added
    line = file.readline()
file.close()
```

This code will print each line of the file, one by one.

2.3 Reading All Lines into a List

The `readlines()` method reads all lines of the file and stores them in a list. Each line becomes an element in the list.

Example:

```python
python
```

```
file = open('data.txt', 'r')
lines = file.readlines()
for line in lines:
    print(line, end='')
file.close()
```

This method is especially useful when you want to process all lines of the file at once.

3. Writing to Files

To write data to a file, you need to open the file in write (`'w'`) or append (`'a'`) mode. Writing in write mode (`'w'`) will overwrite the existing contents of the file, while append mode will add new data to the end.

3.1 Writing a String to a File

You can use the `write()` method to write a string to a file. This method does not add a newline after the string, so if you want to add new lines, you need to include them explicitly.

Example:

python

```
file = open('output.txt', 'w')
file.write('Hello, world!\n')
```

```
file.write('This is a new line.\n')
file.close()
```

This writes two lines to `output.txt`.

3.2 Writing Multiple Lines to a File

To write multiple lines, you can use the `writelines()` method, which takes a list of strings and writes each item in the list as a new line in the file.

Example:

```python
lines = ['First line\n', 'Second line\n', 'Third
line\n']
file = open('output.txt', 'w')
file.writelines(lines)
file.close()
```

This will write three lines to `output.txt`.

4. File Modes: Understanding How Files are Opened

The **mode** in which a file is opened determines how the file is accessed and whether it is read, written to, or appended to. Here is a quick summary of the most commonly used modes:

- `'r'`: **Read mode** – Opens the file for reading. The file must exist.

- `'w'`: **Write mode** – Opens the file for writing. If the file exists, it will be overwritten. If it doesn't exist, it will be created.

- `'a'`: **Append mode** – Opens the file for appending data to the end. If the file doesn't exist, it will be created.

- `'b'`: **Binary mode** – Opens the file in binary mode. Used for reading or writing binary files like images or audio files.

- `'x'`: **Exclusive creation mode** – Opens the file for writing, but the file must not exist. If it exists, Python will raise an error.

- `'rb'`: **Read binary mode** – Used to read binary files (e.g., images, videos).

Hands-On Project: Create a To-Do List App That Saves and Loads Tasks from a File

Let's put our file handling knowledge into practice by building a **to-do list app** that saves and loads tasks from a file. In this project, we'll use file handling to persistently store tasks, so the app's data isn't lost when the program ends.

Step 1: Plan the To-Do List App

Our to-do list app will have the following features:

- **Add a task**: Users can add a new task to the list.
- **View all tasks**: Users can view all the tasks in the list.
- **Delete a task**: Users can delete tasks that are no longer needed.
- **Save and load tasks**: Tasks will be saved to a file when the program ends and loaded when the program starts.

Step 2: Write the Code

python

```python
def load_tasks():
    try:
        with open('tasks.txt', 'r') as file:
            tasks = file.readlines()
        return [task.strip() for task in tasks]
    except FileNotFoundError:
        return []


def save_tasks(tasks):
    with open('tasks.txt', 'w') as file:
        for task in tasks:
            file.write(task + '\n')


def display_tasks(tasks):
```

```python
    if tasks:
        print("\nTo-Do List:")
        for idx, task in enumerate(tasks, 1):
            print(f"{idx}. {task}")
    else:
        print("\nNo tasks found.")


def add_task(tasks):
    task = input("\nEnter the new task: ")
    tasks.append(task)
    save_tasks(tasks)
    print("Task added!")


def delete_task(tasks):
    display_tasks(tasks)
    if tasks:
        try:
            task_num = int(input("\nEnter the task
number to delete: "))
            if 1 <= task_num <= len(tasks):
                removed_task = tasks.pop(task_num -
1)
                save_tasks(tasks)
                print(f"Task '{removed_task}'
deleted.")
            else:
                print("Invalid task number.")
        except ValueError:
            print("Please enter a valid number.")
```

```python
    else:
        print("No tasks to delete.")

def main():
    tasks = load_tasks()

    while True:
        print("\nTo-Do List Menu:")
        print("1. View tasks")
        print("2. Add a task")
        print("3. Delete a task")
        print("4. Exit")

        choice = input("Choose an option: ")

        if choice == '1':
            display_tasks(tasks)
        elif choice == '2':
            add_task(tasks)
        elif choice == '3':
            delete_task(tasks)
        elif choice == '4':
            print("Goodbye!")
            break
        else:
            print("Invalid choice. Please try
again.")

# Run the program
```

`main()`

Step 3: Explanation of the Code

1. **load_tasks():**
   - This function reads tasks from a file called `tasks.txt`. If the file exists, it loads each line as a task. If the file doesn't exist, it returns an empty list.

2. **save_tasks():**
   - This function saves the tasks to the `tasks.txt` file. It writes each task to a new line in the file.

3. **display_tasks():**
   - This function displays all the tasks currently stored in the list.

4. **add_task():**
   - This function prompts the user to input a new task and appends it to the list of tasks. It then saves the updated task list to the file.

5. **delete_task():**
   - This function allows the user to delete a task by selecting its number. After the task is removed, the task list is saved back to the file.

6. **main():**
   - This function handles the user interface, allowing the user to choose between viewing tasks, adding a task, deleting a task, or exiting the program.

Step 4: Testing the To-Do List App

1. **Add tasks**: Run the app, and try adding a few tasks to see if they are saved correctly.

2. **View tasks**: Display the tasks and verify that they appear correctly.

3. **Delete tasks**: Try deleting a task and ensure that the list is updated properly.

Takeaways: How to Save User Data Persistently Using Files

By the end of this chapter, you should be comfortable with the following:

1. **Opening Files**: Using Python's `open()` function to access files for reading and writing.

2. **Reading from Files**: Using methods like `read()`, `readline()`, and `readlines()` to retrieve data from files.

3. **Writing to Files**: Using `write()` and `writelines()` to store data in files.

4. **File Modes**: Understanding the different modes (e.g., `'r'`, `'w'`, `'a'`) for opening files in Python and how they affect file access.

5. **Persisting Data**: Creating applications that save and load user data from files, ensuring that data is not lost when the program ends.

The to-do list project demonstrated how to create a program that interacts with files, allowing users to add, update, and delete tasks while saving the data to a file. This basic file handling capability is foundational for many real-world applications, including data logging, configuration files, and more.

Mastering file handling in Python is a key skill that allows you to build more advanced programs that can store and manage large amounts of data efficiently.

Chapter 7: Object-Oriented Programming (OOP): Basics of Classes and Objects

---

Overview: An Introduction to Object-Oriented Programming Principles in Python

Object-Oriented Programming (OOP) is one of the most powerful paradigms in modern programming. It allows you to structure your code in a way that mirrors the real world, making it easier to understand, maintain, and expand. The core idea of OOP is that you define "objects" that contain both **data** and **functions** that manipulate that data.

In Python, OOP is implemented using **classes** and **objects**. Classes are blueprints for creating objects (instances), and objects are instances of a class. This chapter will introduce you to the basic principles of OOP, including:

- **Classes**: Templates for creating objects that define their structure and behavior.

- **Objects**: Instances of a class that contain specific data.

- **Attributes**: Variables that store data related to an object.

- **Methods**: Functions that define the behavior of an object.

By the end of this chapter, you will have a solid understanding of how to define classes and objects in Python, how to assign data to objects, and how to create behaviors for objects using methods. Additionally, you will apply these principles in a hands-on project where you will build a simple library system.

Topics: Classes, Objects, Methods, and Attributes

1. Classes: Blueprints for Objects

A **class** is essentially a template or blueprint for creating objects. It defines the **attributes** (data) and **methods** (behavior) that the objects created from the class will have. You can think of a class as a **factory** that creates objects, each with its own unique data.

1.1 Defining a Class

To define a class in Python, you use the `class` keyword, followed by the class name (which typically follows the CamelCase convention). The class definition can contain methods and attributes that describe the behavior and state of the objects created from the class.

Syntax:

```python
python

class ClassName:
    def __init__(self, parameters):
        # Constructor to initialize attributes
        self.attribute1 = value
        self.attribute2 = value
```

- `__init__(self, parameters)`: This is the **constructor** of the class. It is a special method that gets called when an object is created from the class. It's used to initialize the attributes of the object.
- `self`: This refers to the instance of the class, allowing access to the object's attributes and methods.

Example:

```python
python

class Car:
    def __init__(self, make, model, year):
        self.make = make
        self.model = model
```

```
self.year = year
```

In this example, `Car` is a class with three attributes: `make`, `model`, and `year`. These attributes are initialized using the `__init__` method when an object is created.

1.2 Instantiating Objects from a Class

Once a class is defined, you can create objects (instances) of that class. When an object is created, the `__init__` method is called to initialize the attributes.

Example:

python

```
my_car = Car("Toyota", "Corolla", 2021)
```

Here, `my_car` is an instance of the `Car` class. The `__init__` method sets the `make`, `model`, and `year` attributes for this specific object.

2. Attributes: Storing Data in Objects

Attributes are variables that belong to an object. They are used to store data related to the object. When you create an object from a class, the attributes store the specific data for that object.

2.1 Defining Attributes

Attributes are usually defined inside the __init__ method, but they can also be added outside of it.

Example:

python

```
class Person:
    def __init__(self, name, age):
        self.name = name
        self.age = age
        self.is_active = True  # Default attribute
```

Here, name and age are attributes that are initialized when an object is created. is_active is an additional attribute that is set to True by default.

2.2 Accessing and Modifying Attributes

You can access and modify the attributes of an object using dot notation.

Example:

python

```
person1 = Person("Alice", 30)
```

```
print(person1.name)   # Output: Alice

person1.age = 31   # Modify the age attribute
print(person1.age)   # Output: 31
```

In this example, we access the `name` attribute of `person1` and change the `age` attribute to `31`.

3. Methods: Defining Behaviors for Objects

A **method** is a function that is defined inside a class and describes the behavior of the object. Methods allow objects to perform actions and interact with other objects.

3.1 Defining Methods

Methods are defined inside the class using the `def` keyword, just like normal functions. The first parameter of every method must be `self`, which refers to the instance of the object.

Example:

python

```
class Dog:
    def __init__(self, name, breed):
        self.name = name
        self.breed = breed
```

```
def bark(self):
    print(f"{self.name} is barking!")
```

In this example, the `Dog` class has an attribute `name` and `breed`, and a method `bark()` that prints a message indicating that the dog is barking.

3.2 Calling Methods

You can call methods on an object using dot notation.

Example:

python

```
dog1 = Dog("Rex", "Golden Retriever")
dog1.bark()   # Output: Rex is barking!
```

Here, the `bark()` method is called on `dog1`, which prints the message.

4. Inheritance: Sharing Behavior Between Classes

One of the most powerful features of OOP is **inheritance**. Inheritance allows one class to inherit the attributes and methods of another class. This promotes code reuse and allows you to create more specialized versions of a general class.

4.1 Creating a Subclass

A subclass is a class that inherits from another class (the parent class). To create a subclass, you specify the parent class in parentheses after the subclass name.

Example:

python

```python
class Animal:
    def __init__(self, name):
        self.name = name

    def speak(self):
        print(f"{self.name} makes a sound.")

class Dog(Animal):
    def speak(self):
        print(f"{self.name} barks.")
```

In this example, Dog is a subclass of Animal. The Dog class inherits the __init__ and speak() methods from the Animal class, but it also overrides the speak() method to make it specific to dogs.

4.2 Using Inherited Methods

You can create objects of the subclass and call methods, just like you would with a regular class.

Example:

```python
python
```

```python
dog = Dog("Buddy")
dog.speak()   # Output: Buddy barks.
```

Here, the `Dog` object calls the overridden `speak()` method.

5. Polymorphism: Multiple Behaviors for Different Classes

Polymorphism allows objects of different classes to be treated as objects of a common parent class. This is useful when you want to define a single method that works across multiple classes.

5.1 Demonstrating Polymorphism

Using polymorphism, you can have multiple classes that implement the same method in different ways.

Example:

```python
python
```

```python
class Cat(Animal):
    def speak(self):
        print(f"{self.name} meows.")


animals = [Dog("Rex"), Cat("Whiskers")]

for animal in animals:
    animal.speak()  # Output: Rex barks. Whiskers
meows.
```

In this example, the `speak()` method behaves differently depending on whether the object is a `Dog` or a `Cat`, even though both classes inherit from `Animal`.

Hands-On Project: Build a Simple Library System with Books as Objects

Now that we've covered the basics of OOP, let's apply these concepts in a practical project. We will build a simple library system where books are represented as objects.

Step 1: Plan the Library System

The library system will have the following features:

- **Add books**: Add books to the library system.
- **View books**: Display a list of all books in the library.
- **Search books**: Search for books by title or author.
- **Remove books**: Remove books from the library.

We will use a **Book** class to represent books and a **Library** class to manage the collection of books.

Step 2: Define the Book Class

python

```python
class Book:
    def __init__(self, title, author, isbn):
        self.title = title
        self.author = author
        self.isbn = isbn

    def __str__(self):
        return f"{self.title} by {self.author} (ISBN: {self.isbn})"
```

- The `Book` class has three attributes: `title`, `author`, and `isbn`.
- The `__str__` method is defined to return a string representation of the book when we print it.

Step 3: Define the Library Class

python

```python
class Library:
    def __init__(self):
        self.books = []

    def add_book(self, book):
        self.books.append(book)

    def remove_book(self, isbn):
        self.books = [book for book in self.books if
book.isbn != isbn]

    def view_books(self):
        if self.books:
            for book in self.books:
                print(book)
        else:
            print("No books in the library.")

    def search_books(self, keyword):
        found_books = [book for book in self.books if
keyword.lower() in book.title.lower() or
keyword.lower() in book.author.lower()]
        if found_books:
            for book in found_books:
                print(book)
        else:
```

```
    print("No books found.")
```

- The `Library` class has an attribute `books`, which is a list that holds all the books in the library.
- The `add_book()` method adds a new book to the library.
- The `remove_book()` method removes a book based on its ISBN.
- The `view_books()` method displays all the books in the library.
- The `search_books()` method searches for books by title or author.

Step 4: Create a Simple User Interface

python

```python
def main():
    library = Library()

    while True:
        print("\nLibrary System")
        print("1. Add Book")
        print("2. View Books")
        print("3. Remove Book")
        print("4. Search Books")
        print("5. Exit")

        choice = input("Enter your choice: ")
```

```python
    if choice == '1':
        title = input("Enter the title of the
book: ")
        author = input("Enter the author of the
book: ")
        isbn = input("Enter the ISBN of the book:
")
        book = Book(title, author, isbn)
        library.add_book(book)
        print("Book added!")

    elif choice == '2':
        library.view_books()

    elif choice == '3':
        isbn = input("Enter the ISBN of the book
to remove: ")
        library.remove_book(isbn)
        print("Book removed!")

    elif choice == '4':
        keyword = input("Enter a title or author
to search for: ")
        library.search_books(keyword)

    elif choice == '5':
        print("Goodbye!")
        break
```

```
        else:
            print("Invalid choice. Please try
again.")

# Run the program
main()
```

Step 5: Testing the Library System

1. **Add books**: Add a few books with different titles and authors.
2. **View books**: Display the list of all books.
3. **Search books**: Try searching for books by title or author.
4. **Remove books**: Test the removal of a book by ISBN.

Takeaways: How to Model Real-World Problems Using OOP

By the end of this chapter, you should have a clear understanding of:

1. **Classes and Objects**: You learned how to define classes, create objects, and organize data and behavior.
2. **Attributes and Methods**: You discovered how to use attributes to store data and methods to define behavior for objects.

3. **Inheritance**: You saw how inheritance allows a class to inherit properties and methods from another class, making code more reusable.

4. **Polymorphism**: You understood how polymorphism allows different classes to implement the same method in different ways.

5. **Hands-on Project**: You applied your knowledge by building a library system using OOP principles, organizing data about books and implementing methods for managing the library.

OOP allows you to structure your code in a way that is modular, reusable, and easier to maintain. By using classes and objects, you can model real-world entities and behaviors more naturally, making your code more intuitive and scalable.

Chapter 8: Error Handling and Debugging: Making Your Code Robust

Overview: Understanding How to Handle Errors and Debug Python Code

No matter how well-written your code is, errors are bound to happen at some point. Whether it's from an unexpected user input, a failed connection to a database, or a logical mistake in your calculations, errors can cause your program to crash or behave unexpectedly.

Error handling and **debugging** are essential skills for any developer. They help you prevent your program from crashing, allow you to detect and correct mistakes, and make your code more **robust** and **resilient** to unexpected situations.

In this chapter, we'll discuss the following key concepts:

- **Try/except blocks**: These blocks help you catch and handle errors gracefully instead of letting your program crash.

- **Debugging techniques**: These methods will help you identify and fix issues in your code.
- **Logging**: This technique allows you to track what's happening in your program and pinpoint problems.

By the end of this chapter, you'll be equipped with the tools you need to handle errors effectively, debug your code, and make your Python programs more reliable.

Topics: Try/Except Blocks, Debugging Techniques, and Logging

1. Error Handling with Try/Except Blocks

In Python, you can handle errors using **try/except** blocks. These blocks allow you to **try** running a block of code, and if an error occurs, Python will **except** it and run an alternative block of code.

1.1 Syntax of Try/Except

The basic syntax of a try/except block looks like this:

```python
try:
    # Code that might cause an error
```

```
except SomeError as e:
    # Code that runs if an error occurs
    print(f"An error occurred: {e}")
```

- **try**: This block contains code that may raise an error.
- **except**: If an error occurs inside the try block, the code inside the except block will run. You can specify the type of error you expect.
- **SomeError**: This is the type of error you want to catch, such as `ZeroDivisionError` or `ValueError`. If you want to catch all errors, you can use `Exception`.

1.2 Catching Specific Errors

You can catch specific types of errors by specifying the error type after `except`. For example:

Example:

python

```
try:
    result = 10 / 0  # This will cause a
ZeroDivisionError
except ZeroDivisionError as e:
    print(f"Cannot divide by zero: {e}")
```

In this example, the program catches the `ZeroDivisionError` and prints a custom message, preventing the program from crashing.

1.3 Catching Multiple Errors

You can catch multiple types of errors using multiple `except` blocks.

Example:

python

```python
try:
    num = int(input("Enter a number: "))
    result = 10 / num
except ValueError as e:
    print(f"Invalid input. Please enter a valid
number: {e}")
except ZeroDivisionError as e:
    print(f"Cannot divide by zero: {e}")
```

In this example, the program handles both `ValueError` (if the user doesn't enter a valid number) and `ZeroDivisionError` (if the user enters 0).

1.4 The Else Clause

The `else` clause can be added to a `try/except` block. The code in the `else` block runs if no errors occur in the `try` block.

Example:

```python
```

```python
try:
    num = int(input("Enter a number: "))
    result = 10 / num
except ZeroDivisionError as e:
    print(f"Cannot divide by zero: {e}")
except ValueError as e:
    print(f"Invalid input. Please enter a valid
number: {e}")
else:
    print(f"Result: {result}")
```

Here, the `else` block prints the result only if no error occurs.

1.5 The Finally Clause

The `finally` block is optional, and it is always executed, whether an error occurs or not. It's useful for cleanup tasks such as closing files or releasing resources.

Example:

```python
```

```python
try:
    file = open("file.txt", "r")
```

```
    content = file.read()
except FileNotFoundError as e:
    print(f"File not found: {e}")
finally:
    file.close()  # Ensures the file is closed even
if an error occurs
```

In this example, the `finally` block ensures that the file is closed regardless of whether an error occurs.

---

2. Debugging Techniques: Finding and Fixing Errors

Debugging is the process of identifying and resolving bugs or issues in your code. As a developer, it's inevitable that you'll encounter bugs that need to be fixed.

2.1 The Print Debugging Method

One of the simplest ways to debug your Python code is to use **print statements**. By printing the value of variables at different points in your program, you can see what's happening and where things might be going wrong.

Example:

```python
python
```

```python
def calculate_sum(a, b):
    print(f"a: {a}, b: {b}")  # Print the values of a
and b
    return a + b

result = calculate_sum(5, "10")
print(result)
```

This will give you insight into what's going wrong, especially when unexpected results appear.

2.2 Using Python's Built-In Debugger: pdb

Python has a built-in debugger called `pdb`. You can use it to step through your code line by line, inspect variables, and evaluate expressions interactively.

To use `pdb`, add the following code where you want to start debugging:

```python
python
```

```python
import pdb
pdb.set_trace()
```

When Python encounters `pdb.set_trace()`, it will pause execution and drop you into an interactive debugging session.

Example:

```python
python

import pdb

def divide(a, b):
    pdb.set_trace()   # Set the breakpoint
    return a / b

result = divide(10, 0)
```

When the program runs, it will stop at `pdb.set_trace()`, and you can type commands like `n` (next), `s` (step into), and `p` (print variable).

2.3 Using IDE Debuggers

Many Integrated Development Environments (IDEs) such as **PyCharm** or **VSCode** provide built-in debugging tools that allow you to visually step through your code, inspect variables, and set breakpoints. These tools offer a more user-friendly way to debug than using `pdb`.

---

3. Logging: Tracking and Troubleshooting Your Code

Logging is an essential tool for tracking the behavior of your code, especially when it's running in production or has multiple users.

Unlike `print()` statements, logging provides a more flexible and persistent way to record messages about your program's execution.

3.1 Using the logging Module

Python's `logging` module allows you to log messages with different severity levels (e.g., DEBUG, INFO, WARNING, ERROR, CRITICAL). Logging is more powerful than printing because you can control the level of detail and direct logs to different outputs, such as files.

Example:

```python
import logging

logging.basicConfig(level=logging.DEBUG,
format="%(asctime)s - %(levelname)s - %(message)s")

logging.debug("This is a debug message.")
logging.info("This is an info message.")
logging.warning("This is a warning message.")
logging.error("This is an error message.")
logging.critical("This is a critical message.")
```

In this example:

- `DEBUG` messages provide detailed information, typically useful for diagnosing problems.

- `INFO` messages provide general information about the program's progress.

- `WARNING` messages indicate a potential issue that doesn't stop the program.

- `ERROR` messages indicate a problem that caused a specific operation to fail.

- `CRITICAL` messages indicate severe issues that could lead to program failure.

3.2 Configuring Logging Output

You can configure the `logging` module to output logs to a file, which is helpful for tracking the program's execution over time.

Example:

```python
```

```python
logging.basicConfig(filename="app.log",
level=logging.DEBUG, format="%(asctime)s -
%(levelname)s - %(message)s")
logging.info("Application started.")
```

In this example, the log messages are written to a file named `app.log` instead of the console.

Hands-On Project: Build a Simple User Input Validation System for Your Calculator Project

In this project, we will add **error handling** to the previously created calculator program, ensuring that user input is validated and that errors are handled gracefully. The goal is to ensure that:

- Users enter valid numbers.
- Division by zero is prevented.
- Invalid input is caught and handled without crashing the program.

Step 1: Update the Calculator with Error Handling

python

```python
def add(a, b):
    return a + b

def subtract(a, b):
    return a - b

def multiply(a, b):
    return a * b
```

```python
def divide(a, b):
    if b == 0:
        raise ValueError("Cannot divide by zero.")
    return a / b

def get_number_input(prompt):
    while True:
        try:
            return float(input(prompt))
        except ValueError:
            print("Invalid input. Please enter a
valid number.")

def calculator():
    print("Welcome to the calculator!")

    while True:
        try:
            print("\nOperations: Add, Subtract,
Multiply, Divide")
            operation = input("Choose an operation
(or type 'exit' to quit): ").lower()

            if operation == 'exit':
                print("Exiting calculator.")
                break

            if operation not in ['add', 'subtract',
'multiply', 'divide']:
```

```python
            print("Invalid operation. Please try
again.")
            continue

        num1 = get_number_input("Enter the first
number: ")
        num2 = get_number_input("Enter the second
number: ")

        if operation == 'add':
            result = add(num1, num2)
        elif operation == 'subtract':
            result = subtract(num1, num2)
        elif operation == 'multiply':
            result = multiply(num1, num2)
        elif operation == 'divide':
            result = divide(num1, num2)

        print(f"The result is: {result}")
    except ValueError as e:
        print(f"Error: {e}")
    except Exception as e:
        print(f"An unexpected error occurred:
{e}")

calculator()
```

Step 2: Explanation of the Code

1. **Function Definitions**: We defined basic arithmetic functions (add, subtract, multiply, divide) to perform the operations.

2. **Input Validation**: The get_number_input function uses a while loop to repeatedly ask for input until the user enters a valid number (i.e., a valid float).

3. **Error Handling**: The try/except blocks handle:

   o **ValueError** for invalid user input, such as entering text instead of numbers.

   o **ZeroDivisionError** is managed inside the divide() function by checking if the denominator is 0.

4. **General Exception Handling**: We also catch any other unexpected errors with a generic except block, ensuring the program doesn't crash.

Takeaways: How to Manage and Troubleshoot Errors Effectively

By the end of this chapter, you should have learned how to:

1. **Handle Errors Using Try/Except Blocks**: You can catch specific errors and handle them gracefully to ensure your program doesn't crash unexpectedly.

2. **Debug Code Using Print Statements and pdb**: You can find and fix bugs in your code using print statements, Python's built-in debugger (`pdb`), or IDE debuggers.

3. **Log Important Information**: You can track the behavior of your programs and record important information using the `logging` module.

4. **Build Robust Applications**: With error handling and debugging tools, you can write more resilient programs that manage user input, handle unexpected situations, and avoid crashes.

Error handling and debugging are critical skills that make your code more **robust**. By applying these techniques, you will be able to create more reliable and user-friendly applications.

Chapter 9: Working with External Libraries: Expanding Python's Capabilities

Overview: An Introduction to Python's Extensive Libraries and How to Use Them

Python is well-known for its simplicity and ease of use, but one of its most powerful features is the vast array of external libraries that are available for use. These libraries offer pre-written code to help you accomplish common tasks, saving you time and effort. Whether you're working with data, web development, machine learning, or APIs, thére is likely a Python library that can help.

External libraries (also known as **third-party libraries**) are collections of modules that provide additional functionality. These libraries allow you to work with databases, process images, interact with web APIs, manipulate data, and much more. Python's package manager, **pip**, is the tool you will use to install these libraries, and many of these packages are available through **PyPI (Python Package Index)**.

In this chapter, we'll walk you through:

- The concept of external libraries and how they can simplify your code.
- How to install and manage libraries using pip.
- How to use one of the most popular libraries, **requests**, to fetch data from the web and build a weather app.

By the end of this chapter, you'll be able to extend Python's capabilities with external libraries and apply them to real-world projects.

Topics: Installing and Using Third-Party Libraries via Pip

1. What are External Libraries and Why Use Them?

External libraries are pre-built collections of Python code that provide functionality beyond the built-in capabilities of the language. These libraries are written by other developers or organizations and are shared for the benefit of the community. The Python Package Index (PyPI) hosts thousands of these libraries, which you can install and use in your own projects.

For example, Python's standard library offers many built-in modules, such as `os` for interacting with the operating system, `math` for mathematical operations, and `datetime` for date and time handling. However, when you need to work with more specialized tasks, you can turn to external libraries.

Advantages of Using External Libraries:

- **Efficiency**: Save time by reusing pre-written, well-tested code instead of building solutions from scratch.
- **Specialized Functionality**: Libraries often solve specific problems, such as web scraping, image manipulation, or machine learning.
- **Community Support**: Popular libraries are often maintained and updated by the community, ensuring that they stay up-to-date with the latest developments.

2. Installing Libraries with pip

The simplest way to install third-party libraries is through `pip`, Python's built-in package manager. **pip** stands for **Pip Installs Packages**, and it allows you to easily download and install packages from PyPI.

Installing a Library: To install a library, use the following command in your terminal or command prompt:

```bash
pip install package_name
```

For example, if you want to install the **requests** library (which is used for making HTTP requests), you can use:

```bash
pip install requests
```

Upgrading a Library: If you already have a library installed but want to update it to the latest version, you can use:

```bash
pip install --upgrade package_name
```

Uninstalling a Library: To uninstall a library you no longer need, use:

```bash
pip uninstall package_name
```

3. Managing Virtual Environments

When working on multiple Python projects, it's common to run into issues where different projects require different versions of the same library. To address this, you can use **virtual environments**.

A virtual environment is a self-contained directory that contains its own version of Python and the libraries installed using `pip`. This allows you to isolate dependencies for each project, avoiding conflicts.

To create a virtual environment:

1. Install the `virtualenv` package (if you don't have it already):

```bash
```

```
pip install virtualenv
```

2. Create a virtual environment in your project directory:

```bash
```

```
virtualenv venv
```

3. Activate the virtual environment:
    o   On Windows:

    ```bash
    ```

    ```
    .\venv\Scripts\activate
    ```

    o   On macOS/Linux:

    ```bash
    ```

```
source venv/bin/activate
```

When the virtual environment is activated, you can install libraries using `pip`, and they will only be available to that project. To deactivate the virtual environment when you're done, simply type:

```
bash
```

```
deactivate
```

4. Searching for Libraries

If you're not sure which library to use, or if you're looking for a specific package, you can search for libraries on PyPI using the `pip search` command.

Example:

```
bash
```

```
pip search "weather"
```

This command will return a list of packages related to "weather" that you can install.

5. Listing Installed Libraries

To see all the libraries installed in your environment (whether global or virtual), use:

```
bash
```

```
pip list
```

This will list the name and version of each installed package.

Hands-On Project: Create a Weather App Using the Requests Library to Fetch Live Data

Now that you understand how to install and manage external libraries, let's put it into practice by building a simple **weather app**. This app will use the **requests** library to fetch live weather data from an online API and display it to the user.

Step 1: Installing the Requests Library

First, we need to install the `requests` library, which will allow us to send HTTP requests to an external API and get data in return. Open your terminal or command prompt and run:

```bash
bash
```

```
pip install requests
```

Step 2: Setting Up the Weather API

To fetch live weather data, we'll use an external API. For this example, we'll use the **OpenWeatherMap API**. You'll need to sign up for a free account on their website to get an API key.

1. Go to OpenWeatherMap.
2. Sign up for an account and get your free API key.
3. Keep your API key handy, as you will need it to make requests to the API.

Step 3: Writing the Code

Here's the code for a simple weather app that fetches the weather for a given city.

```python
python

import requests

# Function to get weather data
def get_weather(city, api_key):
    # OpenWeatherMap API endpoint
```

```python
    url =
f"http://api.openweathermap.org/data/2.5/weather?q={c
ity}&appid={api_key}&units=metric"

    # Send a GET request to the API
    response = requests.get(url)

    # Check if the request was successful
    if response.status_code == 200:
        data = response.json()

        # Extract relevant data from the response
        temperature = data["main"]["temp"]
        description =
data["weather"][0]["description"]
        city_name = data["name"]

        # Return the weather information
        return f"The weather in {city_name} is
{description} with a temperature of {temperature}°C."
    else:
        return "Error: Could not retrieve weather
data."

# Main function
def main():
    api_key = "your_api_key_here"  # Replace with
your actual API key
    city = input("Enter the city: ")
```

```
weather_info = get_weather(city, api_key)
print(weather_info)

# Run the app
main()
```

Step 4: Explanation of the Code

1. **Requests to Fetch Data:**
   o The `requests.get(url)` function sends an HTTP GET request to the OpenWeatherMap API, using the URL constructed with the provided city name and API key.

2. **Handling the Response:**
   o The response from the API is a JSON object. We use `response.json()` to parse it into a Python dictionary.
   o The temperature and weather description are extracted from the response using dictionary keys.

3. **Displaying the Weather:**
   o The weather data is formatted and printed in a human-readable format. If the API call fails, an error message is displayed.

Step 5: Testing the Weather App

1. **Run the Application**:

    o   Run the program and enter a city name.

    o   The program will fetch the weather data from the API and display it in the console.

2. **Example Output**:

    o   **Input:** `London`

    o   **Output:** `The weather in London is light rain with a temperature of 15.3°C.`

Takeaways: How to Extend Python's Functionality with External Libraries

By the end of this chapter, you should have learned:

1. **External Libraries**: How external libraries can extend Python's capabilities by providing ready-made solutions for common tasks, such as making HTTP requests, working with databases, and performing complex calculations.
2. **Installing Libraries with pip**: How to use Python's package manager, `pip`, to install and manage libraries from PyPI.
3. **Using the requests Library**: How to install and use the `requests` library to interact with external APIs and fetch live data.
4. **Building Practical Applications**: How to apply external libraries to real-world problems, like building a weather app that fetches data from an API.

External libraries are a powerful tool in Python development. By learning to leverage them effectively, you can speed up development, solve complex problems with ease, and focus on building your applications rather than reinventing the wheel.

Chapter 10: Building Simple Games with Pygame: Game Development Basics

Overview: An Introduction to Building Games with Python Using the Pygame Library

Python is a versatile language that's not only great for data science, web development, and automation, but also for building **games**. Whether you want to create a simple 2D game or start working on more complex interactive environments, Python has a library that can help you do just that. One of the most popular and powerful libraries for building games in Python is **Pygame**.

Pygame is a free and open-source library designed to make game development easy. It provides tools to work with graphics, sounds, and input devices (like keyboards and mice), which are all crucial components of any game.

In this chapter, we'll explore the following topics:

- **Setting up Pygame**: Installing and configuring the Pygame library.
- **Game Loops**: Understanding the heart of every game – the game loop.
- **Handling Events**: How to handle player input and other events in your game.
- **Simple Animations**: How to add movement and visual feedback to your game.

By the end of this chapter, you'll have built your own version of the classic game **Pong**, learning the fundamentals of game development in Python along the way.

Topics: Pygame Setup, Game Loops, Handling Events, and Simple Animations

1. Setting Up Pygame

Before diving into game development, we need to make sure that Pygame is properly installed and set up. Fortunately, setting up Pygame in Python is simple.

1.1 Installing Pygame

Pygame is easy to install using Python's package manager, **pip**. To get started, simply run the following command in your terminal or command prompt:

```bash
```

```bash
pip install pygame
```

This command will download and install the Pygame library, making it available for use in your projects.

Once installed, you can verify the installation by running the following code to check the version of Pygame:

```python
```

```python
import pygame
print(pygame.__version__)
```

If Pygame is correctly installed, it will print the version number, confirming that everything is set up properly.

1.2 Setting Up Your First Pygame Window

The first thing we need to do in every game is create a window where the game will be displayed. This is done using Pygame's **display** module.

Here's a simple code snippet that initializes Pygame and opens a window:

```python
import pygame

# Initialize Pygame
pygame.init()

# Set up the game window
window = pygame.display.set_mode((800, 600))  # Width
800px, Height 600px
pygame.display.set_caption("My First Game")

# Game loop
running = True
while running:
    for event in pygame.event.get():
        if event.type == pygame.QUIT:
            running = False

# Quit Pygame
```

```
pygame.quit()
```

In this code:

- `pygame.init()` initializes all the Pygame modules required for the game.
- `pygame.display.set_mode((width, height))` creates a window with the specified dimensions.
- `pygame.display.set_caption("Title")` sets the title of the window.
- The **game loop** keeps the window open and listens for events (like closing the window).

When you run this code, a window will appear with the title "My First Game," and it will remain open until you close it.

2. Game Loops: The Heart of Every Game

A **game loop** is the central part of any game. It is the loop that keeps the game running, updating the game state, rendering graphics, and processing user inputs continuously. Without the game loop, your game wouldn't be interactive.

The basic structure of a game loop involves:

- **Handling events**: Responding to user input, like keyboard presses or mouse clicks.

- **Updating the game state**: Changing the positions of game objects, updating scores, and other in-game events.
- **Drawing the screen**: Redrawing the screen with updated information.
- **Frame rate control**: Ensuring the game runs at a consistent speed.

2.1 Structuring the Game Loop

Here's a simplified version of a game loop:

python

```python
import pygame

# Initialize Pygame
pygame.init()

# Set up the game window
window = pygame.display.set_mode((800, 600))
pygame.display.set_caption("Game Loop Example")

# Game loop
running = True
while running:
    # Handle events
    for event in pygame.event.get():
        if event.type == pygame.QUIT:
```

```
        running = False

    # Update game state (this could be moving
objects, etc.)

    # Draw to the screen (clear screen and draw
objects)
    window.fill((0, 0, 0))  # Fill screen with black
color

    # Refresh the display
    pygame.display.update()

# Quit Pygame
pygame.quit()
```

In this basic loop:

- **Handling events** is done through `pygame.event.get()` to catch all events (like the window close event).
- **Updating the game state** and **drawing** happen inside the loop.
- The screen is refreshed using `pygame.display.update()` to display the changes.

3. Handling Events: Responding to User Input

One of the main aspects of game programming is handling user input, whether it's from a keyboard, mouse, or other devices. Pygame makes it easy to handle input events.

3.1 Handling Keyboard Events

To respond to keyboard inputs, we can check the state of the keys in the game loop using `pygame.key.get_pressed()`. This method returns a list of boolean values representing the state (pressed or not) of each key on the keyboard.

Here's an example of handling arrow key inputs to move a rectangle:

```python
import pygame

# Initialize Pygame
pygame.init()

# Set up the game window
window = pygame.display.set_mode((800, 600))
pygame.display.set_caption("Move the Rectangle")

# Rectangle properties
rect_x, rect_y = 400, 300
```

```python
rect_width, rect_height = 50, 50
rect_speed = 5

# Game loop
running = True
while running:
    for event in pygame.event.get():
        if event.type == pygame.QUIT:
            running = False

    # Handle key events
    keys = pygame.key.get_pressed()
    if keys[pygame.K_LEFT]:
        rect_x -= rect_speed
    if keys[pygame.K_RIGHT]:
        rect_x += rect_speed
    if keys[pygame.K_UP]:
        rect_y -= rect_speed
    if keys[pygame.K_DOWN]:
        rect_y += rect_speed

    # Draw to the screen
    window.fill((0, 0, 0))  # Clear the screen with
black color
    pygame.draw.rect(window, (255, 0, 0), (rect_x,
rect_y, rect_width, rect_height))  # Draw the
rectangle

    # Refresh the display
```

```
    pygame.display.update()
```

```
pygame.quit()
```

In this example, the `pygame.key.get_pressed()` method checks whether the arrow keys are pressed and updates the position of the rectangle accordingly.

3.2 Handling Mouse Events

Pygame also provides ways to handle mouse input. You can track mouse movements, clicks, and get the mouse's position.

Here's an example of how to track mouse clicks:

python

```python
import pygame

# Initialize Pygame
pygame.init()

# Set up the game window
window = pygame.display.set_mode((800, 600))
pygame.display.set_caption("Mouse Click Example")

# Game loop
running = True
while running:
```

```
    for event in pygame.event.get():
        if event.type == pygame.QUIT:
            running = False
        if event.type == pygame.MOUSEBUTTONDOWN:
            mouse_x, mouse_y = pygame.mouse.get_pos()
            print(f"Mouse clicked at: ({mouse_x},
{mouse_y})")

pygame.quit()
```

In this code, `pygame.MOUSEBUTTONDOWN` detects when the mouse is clicked, and `pygame.mouse.get_pos()` gets the position of the mouse.

4. Simple Animations: Adding Movement and Visual Feedback

Animations are a crucial part of any game. They make your game interactive and visually engaging. In Pygame, animations are created by moving objects around the screen and refreshing the display at regular intervals.

4.1 Moving Objects and Animating

In this example, we'll animate a square moving across the screen:

```
python
```

```
import pygame
```

```
# Initialize Pygame
pygame.init()

# Set up the game window
window = pygame.display.set_mode((800, 600))
pygame.display.set_caption("Simple Animation")

# Square properties
x, y = 0, 300
width, height = 50, 50
speed = 5

# Game loop
running = True
while running:
    for event in pygame.event.get():
        if event.type == pygame.QUIT:
            running = False

    # Move the square
    x += speed
    if x > 800:  # Reset to the left when it moves
off the screen
        x = -width

    # Draw to the screen
    window.fill((0, 0, 0))  # Clear the screen with
black
```

```
    pygame.draw.rect(window, (255, 0, 0), (x, y,
width, height))  # Draw the square

    # Refresh the display
    pygame.display.update()

pygame.quit()
```

In this example, the square moves from left to right across the screen. When it moves off the screen, it resets to the left side and starts again.

Hands-On Project: Create a Basic Version of the Classic Game "Pong"

Now, let's put everything together and build a simple version of the classic **Pong** game. This game will include the following features:

- Two paddles (one for each player).
- A bouncing ball.
- Basic controls for player movement.
- Scoring system.

Step 1: Set Up the Game Window

Start by setting up the basic window and defining the dimensions of the paddles and ball.

```python
python

import pygame
import random

# Initialize Pygame
pygame.init()

# Set up the game window
window = pygame.display.set_mode((800, 600))
pygame.display.set_caption("Pong")

# Colors
WHITE = (255, 255, 255)
BLACK = (0, 0, 0)

# Paddle dimensions
paddle_width = 15
paddle_height = 100
ball_radius = 10

# Initial positions of paddles and ball
left_paddle_y = 250
right_paddle_y = 250
ball_x = 400
ball_y = 300
ball_speed_x = random.choice([5, -5])
ball_speed_y = random.choice([5, -5])
```

```python
# Speed of paddles
paddle_speed = 10

# Game loop
running = True
while running:
    for event in pygame.event.get():
        if event.type == pygame.QUIT:
            running = False

    # Handling paddle movement
    keys = pygame.key.get_pressed()
    if keys[pygame.K_w] and left_paddle_y > 0:
        left_paddle_y -= paddle_speed
    if keys[pygame.K_s] and left_paddle_y < 600 -
paddle_height:
        left_paddle_y += paddle_speed
    if keys[pygame.K_UP] and right_paddle_y > 0:
        right_paddle_y -= paddle_speed
    if keys[pygame.K_DOWN] and right_paddle_y < 600 -
paddle_height:
        right_paddle_y += paddle_speed

    # Ball movement
    ball_x += ball_speed_x
    ball_y += ball_speed_y

    # Ball collision with top and bottom
    if ball_y <= 0 or ball_y >= 600 - ball_radius:
```

```
        ball_speed_y *= -1


    # Ball collision with paddles
    if (ball_x <= paddle_width and left_paddle_y <=
ball_y <= left_paddle_y + paddle_height) or \
        (ball_x >= 800 - paddle_width - ball_radius
and right_paddle_y <= ball_y <= right_paddle_y +
paddle_height):
        ball_speed_x *= -1


    # Ball out of bounds
    if ball_x < 0 or ball_x > 800:
        ball_x = 400  # Reset the ball
        ball_y = 300
        ball_speed_x *= random.choice([1, -1])
        ball_speed_y *= random.choice([1, -1])


    # Drawing to the screen
    window.fill(BLACK)
    pygame.draw.rect(window, WHITE, (0,
left_paddle_y, paddle_width, paddle_height))  # Left
paddle
    pygame.draw.rect(window, WHITE, (785,
right_paddle_y, paddle_width, paddle_height))  #
Right paddle
    pygame.draw.circle(window, WHITE, (ball_x,
ball_y), ball_radius)  # Ball


    # Refresh the display
```

```
    pygame.display.update()
```

```
pygame.quit()
```

Step 2: Adding Scoring and Game Over

Next, let's add a scoring system and game over functionality. We'll increase the score whenever the ball goes past a paddle and reset the ball to the center.

python

```python
# Score variables
left_score = 0
right_score = 0
font = pygame.font.SysFont("Arial", 32)

# Game loop
running = True
while running:
    for event in pygame.event.get():
        if event.type == pygame.QUIT:
            running = False

    # Handling paddle movement
    keys = pygame.key.get_pressed()
    if keys[pygame.K_w] and left_paddle_y > 0:
        left_paddle_y -= paddle_speed
    if keys[pygame.K_s] and left_paddle_y < 600 -
paddle_height:
```

```python
        left_paddle_y += paddle_speed
    if keys[pygame.K_UP] and right_paddle_y > 0:
        right_paddle_y -= paddle_speed
    if keys[pygame.K_DOWN] and right_paddle_y < 600 -
paddle_height:
        right_paddle_y += paddle_speed

    # Ball movement
    ball_x += ball_speed_x
    ball_y += ball_speed_y

    # Ball collision with top and bottom
    if ball_y <= 0 or ball_y >= 600 - ball_radius:
        ball_speed_y *= -1

    # Ball collision with paddles
    if (ball_x <= paddle_width and left_paddle_y <=
ball_y <= left_paddle_y + paddle_height) or \
        (ball_x >= 800 - paddle_width - ball_radius
and right_paddle_y <= ball_y <= right_paddle_y +
paddle_height):
        ball_speed_x *= -1

    # Ball out of bounds
    if ball_x < 0:
        right_score += 1
        ball_x = 400  # Reset the ball
        ball_y = 300
        ball_speed_x *= random.choice([1, -1])
```

```
        ball_speed_y *= random.choice([1, -1])
    elif ball_x > 800:
        left_score += 1
        ball_x = 400  # Reset the ball
        ball_y = 300
        ball_speed_x *= random.choice([1, -1])
        ball_speed_y *= random.choice([1, -1])


    # Draw the score
    score_text = font.render(f"{left_score} -
{right_score}", True, WHITE)
    window.blit(score_text, (350, 10))


    # Drawing to the screen
    window.fill(BLACK)
    pygame.draw.rect(window, WHITE, (0,
left_paddle_y, paddle_width, paddle_height))  # Left
paddle
    pygame.draw.rect(window, WHITE, (785,
right_paddle_y, paddle_width, paddle_height))  #
Right paddle
    pygame.draw.circle(window, WHITE, (ball_x,
ball_y), ball_radius)  # Ball


    # Refresh the display
    pygame.display.update()

pygame.quit()
```

Step 3: Running and Playing the Game

You can now run the game and start playing. The ball will bounce between the paddles, and the score will increase when the ball goes past a paddle. The game will continue until you close the window.

Takeaways: How to Get Started with Game Development in Python

By the end of this chapter, you should have learned how to:

1. **Set Up Pygame**: Install and configure Pygame for game development.
2. **Game Loops**: Understand the game loop and its importance in keeping the game interactive and running.
3. **Handle Events**: Handle user input, such as keyboard and mouse events, to control game objects.
4. **Create Animations**: Add movement and visual feedback to the game by animating objects.
5. **Build a Simple Game**: Apply these concepts by creating a basic Pong game with scoring and simple gameplay mechanics.

Pygame is an incredibly useful library that can help you bring your game development ideas to life. Whether you're creating a simple 2D game or planning something more complex, Pygame offers the tools you need to build interactive and engaging experiences.

Chapter 11: Building a To-Do List App: Practical Application of Concepts

---

Overview: Putting Together Multiple Python Concepts in a Real-World Application

As you progress in your Python journey, one of the most valuable skills is being able to apply multiple programming concepts into one project. A real-world project helps solidify your understanding of various Python concepts and shows you how they work together.

In this chapter, we will combine several key concepts in Python to build a practical application—a **to-do list app**. This project will cover:

- **Object-Oriented Programming (OOP)** to manage tasks.
- **File Handling** to save tasks to a file and ensure data persists across app sessions.
- **User Input** to allow the user to interact with the app, add, edit, and delete tasks.

By the end of this chapter, you will not only have built a functional to-do list app but also gained experience in integrating various Python concepts into a single project. This is an essential step toward mastering Python and applying it to real-world applications.

Topics: Combining OOP, File Handling, and User Input

1. Object-Oriented Programming (OOP) for Task Management

In the to-do list app, we will use **Object-Oriented Programming (OOP)** to model the main concept of a task. OOP allows us to define a class that represents a task, with attributes such as **task name**, **status** (completed or pending), and **due date**.

1.1 Defining the Task Class

Let's define the `Task` class that will represent a task in our to-do list. This class will have attributes like `name`, `status`, and `due_date`. We will also include methods to **mark a task as completed** and **display the task details**.

python

```python
class Task:
    def __init__(self, name, due_date):
```

```python
        self.name = name
        self.status = "Pending"  # Default status is
"Pending"
        self.due_date = due_date

    def mark_as_completed(self):
        self.status = "Completed"

    def __str__(self):
        return f"Task: {self.name}, Due Date:
{self.due_date}, Status: {self.status}"
```

- **__init__ Method**: This is the constructor, where we initialize the task's name, status, and due date.
- **mark_as_completed Method**: This method changes the status of a task to "Completed".
- **__str__ Method**: This method returns a formatted string for displaying the task's details.

1.2 Managing Multiple Tasks

Next, we will create a `ToDoList` class that will manage a list of tasks. This class will allow us to add tasks, edit tasks, delete tasks, and display all tasks.

python

```python
class ToDoList:
```

```python
def __init__(self):
    self.tasks = []  # List to store tasks

def add_task(self, task):
    self.tasks.append(task)

def remove_task(self, task_name):
    for task in self.tasks:
        if task.name == task_name:
            self.tasks.remove(task)
            return True
    return False

def edit_task(self, old_name, new_name,
new_due_date):
    for task in self.tasks:
        if task.name == old_name:
            task.name = new_name
            task.due_date = new_due_date
            return True
    return False

def display_tasks(self):
    if not self.tasks:
        print("No tasks available.")
    for task in self.tasks:
        print(task)

def save_tasks_to_file(self, filename):
```

```
        with open(filename, 'w') as file:
            for task in self.tasks:

file.write(f"{task.name},{task.due_date},{task.status
}\n")


    def load_tasks_from_file(self, filename):
        try:
            with open(filename, 'r') as file:
                for line in file:
                    name, due_date, status =
line.strip().split(',')
                    task = Task(name, due_date)
                    if status == "Completed":
                        task.mark_as_completed()
                    self.add_task(task)
        except FileNotFoundError:
            print("No previous tasks found.")
```

- **add_task Method**: Adds a task to the list of tasks.
- **remove_task Method**: Removes a task from the list by its name.
- **edit_task Method**: Edits an existing task's name and due date.
- **display_tasks Method**: Displays all the tasks in the to-do list.
- **save_tasks_to_file Method**: Saves the current tasks to a file.

- **`load_tasks_from_file` Method**: Loads tasks from a file when the program starts.

2. File Handling: Saving and Loading Data

File handling is essential for saving the tasks in our to-do list so that they persist between app sessions. In the `ToDoList` class, we've implemented methods to **save tasks to a file** and **load tasks from a file**.

2.1 Saving Tasks to a File

We use Python's built-in `open()` function to open a file for writing and save the task data. Each task is saved as a comma-separated string, containing the task's name, due date, and status.

python

```python
with open(filename, 'w') as file:
    for task in self.tasks:

file.write(f"{task.name},{task.due_date},{task.status}\n")
```

This code writes each task's details to a file, one task per line. Each attribute is separated by a comma for easy parsing when loading the file.

2.2 Loading Tasks from a File

When the user starts the app, we'll load the tasks from a file using the `load_tasks_from_file` method. This method opens the file for reading, parses each line to create a `Task` object, and adds it to the list of tasks.

python

```
with open(filename, 'r') as file:
    for line in file:
        name, due_date, status =
line.strip().split(',')
        task = Task(name, due_date)
        if status == "Completed":
            task.mark_as_completed()
        self.add_task(task)
```

The `split()` method separates the attributes from the comma-separated string, and we create a new `Task` object for each line. If the status is "Completed", we call the `mark_as_completed()` method.

3. Handling User Input: Adding, Editing, and Deleting Tasks

Now that we've defined the main structure of our to-do list app using OOP and file handling, we need to allow users to interact with the app. The app should allow the user to:

- **Add tasks**
- **Edit tasks**
- **Delete tasks**
- **View tasks**

3.1 User Interface for Adding Tasks

We can use the `input()` function to collect user input and add tasks to the to-do list.

python

```
def add_task_prompt(todo_list):
    name = input("Enter the task name: ")
    due_date = input("Enter the due date (YYYY-MM-
DD): ")
    task = Task(name, due_date)
    todo_list.add_task(task)
    print("Task added successfully.")
```

This function prompts the user for a task name and due date, creates a new `Task` object, and adds it to the `ToDoList` object.

3.2 User Interface for Editing Tasks

To edit an existing task, the user needs to specify the name of the task they want to change, as well as the new name and due date.

python

```python
def edit_task_prompt(todo_list):
    old_name = input("Enter the name of the task to edit: ")
    new_name = input("Enter the new task name: ")
    new_due_date = input("Enter the new due date (YYYY-MM-DD): ")
    if todo_list.edit_task(old_name, new_name, new_due_date):
        print("Task updated successfully.")
    else:
        print("Task not found.")
```

This function allows the user to edit a task by changing its name and due date.

3.3 User Interface for Deleting Tasks

Deleting a task is simple: the user provides the name of the task they want to remove, and the app deletes it.

python

```python
def delete_task_prompt(todo_list):
    name = input("Enter the name of the task to delete: ")
    if todo_list.remove_task(name):
        print("Task deleted successfully.")
```

```
    else:
        print("Task not found.")
```

This function allows the user to remove a task from the list by specifying its name.

3.4 User Interface for Viewing Tasks

Finally, the user can view all tasks in the list with a simple function call.

python

```
def view_tasks_prompt(todo_list):
    todo_list.display_tasks()
```

This function simply calls the `display_tasks()` method from the `ToDoList` class to print all the tasks in the list.

4. Putting Everything Together

Now, let's combine everything into the main program. We'll allow the user to choose what action they want to perform (add, edit, delete, view), and the program will respond accordingly.

python

```
def main():
    todo_list = ToDoList()
```

```python
    todo_list.load_tasks_from_file("tasks.txt")

while True:
    print("\nTo-Do List App")
    print("1. Add Task")
    print("2. Edit Task")
    print("3. Delete Task")
    print("4. View Tasks")
    print("5. Save and Exit")

    choice = input("Choose an option: ")

    if choice == "1":
        add_task_prompt(todo_list)
    elif choice == "2":
        edit_task_prompt(todo_list)
    elif choice == "3":
        delete_task_prompt(todo_list)
    elif choice == "4":
        view_tasks_prompt(todo_list)
    elif choice == "5":
        todo_list.save_tasks_to_file("tasks.txt")
        print("Tasks saved. Goodbye!")
        break
    else:
        print("Invalid choice. Please try
again.")

# Run the application
```

```
main()
```

In this `main()` function:

- We create an instance of the `ToDoList` class.
- We load existing tasks from the `tasks.txt` file.
- We present a menu to the user and allow them to add, edit, delete, or view tasks.
- When the user chooses to exit, we save all tasks back to the file.

Step 5: Testing the To-Do List App

Now, you can run the program and test all the features:

1. **Add tasks** and check if they are displayed correctly.
2. **Edit tasks** and verify that the changes are saved.
3. **Delete tasks** and make sure they are removed from the list.
4. **View tasks** and confirm that the tasks are displayed as expected.

Takeaways: Learn How to Integrate Various Python Concepts into One Project

By the end of this chapter, you should have a solid understanding of:

1. **Object-Oriented Programming (OOP)**: You learned how to model real-world objects, such as tasks, using classes and methods.

2. **File Handling**: You learned how to use file handling to save and load data, ensuring that the to-do list is persistent across app sessions.

3. **User Input**: You learned how to handle user input to create an interactive app that allows users to add, edit, delete, and view tasks.

Building a to-do list app is a great exercise for integrating multiple Python concepts into a single project. It demonstrates how to use OOP, file handling, and user input together to create a practical, functional application.

With these skills, you can tackle more complex projects, like inventory systems, task managers, or even simple games. This project serves as a solid foundation for understanding how different parts of Python work together in real-world applications.

Chapter 12: Introduction to Microservices: Structuring Scalable Applications

---

Overview: Learn the Basics of Microservices and How Python Can Be Used to Create Scalable Systems

In today's world of software development, building scalable and maintainable applications is more important than ever. One architectural approach that has gained significant traction in recent years is **microservices**. Microservices are an approach to software development where a large application is divided into smaller, independently deployable services, each responsible for a specific piece of functionality.

The microservices architecture is fundamentally different from the **monolithic architecture**, where all components of an application are tightly coupled and function as a single unit. In a microservices-based application, each service is independently developed, deployed, and scaled, allowing for a more flexible and robust system.

In this chapter, we'll dive into:

- **What microservices are**: A comprehensive look at the microservices architecture.
- **How they are structured**: How to break down an application into smaller services.
- **How to communicate between them**: Using APIs (Application Programming Interfaces) to enable services to interact with each other.

By the end of this chapter, you will have hands-on experience in creating a **basic microservice** for a bookstore application, which handles **book inventory** and **orders**.

Topics: What Microservices Are, How They Are Structured, and How to Communicate Between Them Using APIs

1. What are Microservices?

Microservices is an architectural style where an application is composed of loosely coupled, independently deployable services.

Each service in the system is small, focused on a specific business capability, and communicates with other services over a network, typically using HTTP or messaging queues.

A microservices architecture offers several advantages:

- **Scalability**: You can scale services independently based on demand.
- **Flexibility**: Developers can use different programming languages and technologies for different services.
- **Resilience**: Failures in one service do not necessarily affect others.
- **Maintainability**: Smaller, focused services are easier to maintain, update, and test.

In a traditional monolithic application, all components are tightly integrated into a single codebase. In contrast, in a microservices architecture, the application is decomposed into small, self-contained services that interact with each other.

Key Characteristics of Microservices:

1. **Single Responsibility**: Each microservice is designed to perform a specific task or manage a particular domain of the application.

2. **Decentralized Data Management**: Each microservice manages its own database or data storage, ensuring that services are loosely coupled and can be scaled independently.

3. **Communication via APIs**: Microservices typically communicate using RESTful APIs or messaging systems like RabbitMQ or Kafka.

4. **Independent Deployment**: Microservices can be deployed independently, meaning updates to one service can be done without affecting other services.

2. Structuring Microservices

In a microservices architecture, the application is broken down into smaller services, each responsible for a particular functionality. Here's an overview of how to structure these services:

2.1 Decomposing the Application

When designing microservices, the first step is to identify the **business domains** or functionalities that can be separated into individual services. For example, consider an e-commerce application:

- **Inventory Service**: Handles the management of products, their stock quantities, etc.

- **Order Service**: Handles customer orders, including processing payments, shipping, etc.
- **User Service**: Handles user authentication, registration, and profile management.
- **Shipping Service**: Manages logistics and order shipping.

Each of these components is a **microservice** that runs independently. They interact with each other through APIs.

2.2 Communication Between Microservices

Microservices communicate over HTTP, most commonly using **RESTful APIs**. Each microservice exposes its own API that other services can call. This is typically done using **JSON** as the data format.

For example, the `Inventory Service` might expose an endpoint to get a list of available products:

```
http
```

```
GET /api/products
```

Other services, such as the `Order Service`, can call this API to retrieve product details when a customer places an order.

2.3 Decentralized Data Management

Each microservice typically manages its own **data store**. For example, the `Inventory Service` might use a database to store product information, while the `Order Service` uses its own database to store order details. This decentralized approach helps in scaling and ensures that services remain loosely coupled.

3. Communication Between Microservices Using APIs

Now that we understand the general structure of microservices, it's important to learn how services communicate with each other. The most common method of communication is through **APIs**, typically REST APIs.

3.1 RESTful APIs

REST (Representational State Transfer) is an architectural style for designing networked applications. A RESTful API is one that follows the principles of REST:

- **Stateless**: Each API request contains all the information needed for processing, and no session information is stored between requests.

- **HTTP Methods**: RESTful APIs use standard HTTP methods such as GET, POST, PUT, and DELETE to interact with resources.
- **Resource-based**: Resources are identified by URLs, and each resource can have different representations (typically in JSON format).

Here's a simple example of how two microservices might communicate using REST APIs:

1. **Inventory Service**: Exposes an API to check the stock of a book.
   - `GET /api/books/{book_id}/stock`
2. **Order Service**: Calls the Inventory Service's API to check stock when placing an order.

Example in Python using the `requests` library:

```python
python

import requests

def check_stock(book_id):
    url = f"http://inventory-service/api/books/{book_id}/stock"
    response = requests.get(url)
    if response.status_code == 200:
        return response.json()['stock']
```

```
    else:
        return "Error fetching stock information"
```

This simple function calls the `Inventory Service`'s API to check the stock of a book.

3.2 Handling Errors and Retries

Microservices often need to communicate over the network, and sometimes things go wrong. Errors such as timeouts, server crashes, and network failures are common. A good microservices architecture needs to handle such issues gracefully, usually by implementing **retry mechanisms** and **fallbacks**.

Example: If the `Inventory Service` is down, we can use a retry mechanism to call it again after a short delay.

python

```python
import time
import requests

def check_stock_with_retry(book_id, retries=3):
    url = f"http://inventory-service/api/books/{book_id}/stock"

    for _ in range(retries):
        try:
```

```
            response = requests.get(url, timeout=5)
            if response.status_code == 200:
                return response.json()['stock']
            else:
                print("Error fetching stock
information")
                time.sleep(2)  # Wait before retrying
        except requests.exceptions.RequestException
as e:
            print(f"Error occurred: {e}")
            time.sleep(2)  # Wait before retrying


    return "Could not fetch stock information after
retries"
```

This function attempts to fetch stock information from the
`Inventory Service`, retrying a few times in case of failure.

Hands-On Project: Build a Basic Microservice for a Bookstore That Handles Book Inventory and Orders

Now that we have covered the basic principles of microservices, it's time to put those concepts into practice. Let's build a basic bookstore system with two microservices:

- **Inventory Service**: Manages book inventory (adding and checking stock).
- **Order Service**: Manages customer orders.

In this project, we will use **Flask**, a lightweight Python web framework, to create these microservices.

Step 1: Setting Up Flask for the Microservices

First, you need to install Flask:

bash

```
pip install flask
```

Now, let's create the `Inventory Service` and `Order Service`.

Step 2: Building the Inventory Service

Create a file called `inventory_service.py`:

python

```
from flask import Flask, jsonify, request

app = Flask(__name__)

# In-memory data store (usually you'd use a database)
books_inventory = {
```

```
    "1": {"title": "Python 101", "stock": 50},
    "2": {"title": "Learning Flask", "stock": 30}
}


@app.route('/api/books/<book_id>/stock',
methods=['GET'])
def get_stock(book_id):
    if book_id in books_inventory:
        return jsonify(books_inventory[book_id]), 200
    return jsonify({"error": "Book not found"}), 404


@app.route('/api/books/<book_id>/stock',
methods=['POST'])
def update_stock(book_id):
    if book_id in books_inventory:
        data = request.get_json()
        books_inventory[book_id]["stock"] +=
data.get("quantity", 0)
        return jsonify({"message": "Stock updated
successfully"}), 200
    return jsonify({"error": "Book not found"}), 404


if __name__ == '__main__':
    app.run(port=5001)
```

This simple API allows us to:

- **GET** the stock of a specific book.
- **POST** to update the stock of a specific book.

Step 3: Building the Order Service

Create a file called `order_service.py`:

python

```python
from flask import Flask, jsonify, request
import requests

app = Flask(__name__)

INVENTORY_URL =
"http://localhost:5001/api/books/{}/stock"

@app.route('/api/orders', methods=['POST'])
def create_order():
    data = request.get_json()
    book_id = data['book_id']
    quantity = data['quantity']

    # Check if the book is in stock
    stock_response =
requests.get(INVENTORY_URL.format(book_id))
    if stock_response.status_code == 200:
        stock = stock_response.json()['stock']
        if stock >= quantity:
            # Process the order
            # In a real application, here we'd update
a database and confirm the order
```

```
        return jsonify({"message": "Order placed
successfully"}), 201
        else:
            return jsonify({"error": "Not enough
stock"}), 400
    else:
        return jsonify({"error": "Book not found"}),
404


if __name__ == '__main__':
    app.run(port=5002)
```

The Order Service has a single endpoint for creating orders. It checks the inventory of the book by calling the Inventory Service API.

Step 4: Running the Microservices

1. Start the **Inventory Service**:

bash

```
python inventory_service.py
```

2. Start the **Order Service**:

bash

```
python order_service.py
```

Step 5: Testing the Microservices

To test the services, you can use **Postman** or **cURL** to simulate requests.

1. **Adding Stock**:
    o   Send a `POST` request to `http://localhost:5001/api/books/1/stock` with a JSON body like:

```json
{
    "quantity": 20
}
```

2. **Creating an Order**:
    o   Send a `POST` request to `http://localhost:5002/api/orders` with a JSON body like:

```json
{
    "book_id": "1",
    "quantity": 5
}
```

If there's enough stock, the order will be placed successfully.

Takeaways: How to Structure a Simple Application Using Microservices in Python

By the end of this chapter, you should have gained the following knowledge:

1. **What Microservices Are**: An understanding of microservices, including their advantages, structure, and communication methods using APIs.
2. **How to Structure Microservices**: How to decompose an application into smaller, independent services.
3. **Communication Between Microservices**: How to use RESTful APIs to enable communication between services.
4. **Building Simple Microservices**: How to create basic microservices using Flask, demonstrating how to handle inventory and orders in a bookstore system.
5. **File Handling in Microservices**: While not explored in-depth here, many microservices work with external storage solutions like databases. You can apply similar file handling concepts for persistence.

Microservices allow you to scale your application efficiently and manage each part independently, which is vital for building large-scale systems. Python, combined with frameworks like Flask, makes it easy to implement microservices architecture in a structured and manageable way.

Chapter 13: APIs and Web Scraping: Accessing Data from the Web

Overview: Learn How to Interact with APIs and Scrape Web Data

One of Python's greatest strengths lies in its ability to fetch and manipulate data from the web. Whether you're pulling data from a public API, scraping a website for information, or both, Python offers the tools to make the process smooth and efficient. In this chapter, we'll cover how to interact with **APIs** and how to **scrape web data** using **BeautifulSoup**.

By the end of this chapter, you'll know how to:

- **Fetch data from APIs** using Python, parse JSON responses, and work with the data.
- **Scrape web data** using BeautifulSoup, a powerful library that allows you to extract data from HTML content.

- Use these techniques to build a program that fetches live data, specifically **news headlines** from a public API.

This chapter will show you the power of integrating external web sources into your Python applications, which can enhance the functionality of your projects and help you build real-time applications.

Topics: Fetching Data from APIs, Parsing JSON, Web Scraping with BeautifulSoup

1. Working with APIs: Fetching Data from the Web

APIs (Application Programming Interfaces) are a set of rules that allow different software applications to communicate with each other. Many websites and services provide APIs that allow you to access their data programmatically.

1.1 What is an API?

An **API** is a set of **endpoints** that enable developers to interact with a system's data or features. APIs can be used for many different tasks, including:

- Retrieving weather data.

- Fetching news headlines.
- Managing user accounts.
- Accessing data from a database.

When interacting with an API, you typically send an HTTP request to an endpoint, and the API responds with data, usually in **JSON** format. This data can then be parsed and used in your application.

1.2 How to Fetch Data from an API in Python

Python provides several libraries to make HTTP requests, including `requests`, which is one of the most widely used. To interact with an API, you typically perform a **GET** request, which asks the API for data.

To get started, you need to install the `requests` library:

```bash
bash
```

```bash
pip install requests
```

Here's an example of how to fetch data from a public API:

```python
python
```

```python
import requests

# API endpoint
url = "https://jsonplaceholder.typicode.com/posts"
```

```
# Send a GET request to the API
response = requests.get(url)

# Check if the request was successful
if response.status_code == 200:
    data = response.json()  # Parse the JSON data
from the response
    print(data)
else:
    print(f"Failed to retrieve data. Status code:
{response.status_code}")
```

In this code:

- We use the `requests.get()` method to send a GET request to the API.
- If the request is successful (`status_code == 200`), we use `response.json()` to parse the JSON data into a Python dictionary.
- If the request fails, we print the HTTP status code to understand what went wrong.

1.3 Understanding JSON

JSON (JavaScript Object Notation) is a lightweight data format commonly used for transmitting data between a client and server.

JSON is easy to read, write, and parse, making it a popular choice for APIs.

Here's an example of JSON data returned from an API:

json

```json
[
    {
        "userId": 1,
        "id": 1,
        "title": "My first post",
        "body": "This is the body of the first post."
    },
    {
        "userId": 1,
        "id": 2,
        "title": "My second post",
        "body": "This is the body of the second post."
    }
]
```

The data above is a list of objects, where each object represents a post with properties like userId, id, title, and body.

1.4 Parsing JSON in Python

When you use `response.json()`, it converts the JSON data into Python data types such as lists, dictionaries, and strings.

Here's how you can access specific data from the response:

python

```
import requests

url = "https://jsonplaceholder.typicode.com/posts"
response = requests.get(url)

if response.status_code == 200:
    data = response.json()
    # Print the title of the first post
    print(data[0]['title'])
else:
    print(f"Error: {response.status_code}")
```

This code retrieves the **title** of the first post from the JSON response.

2. Web Scraping with BeautifulSoup

Sometimes, you may want to fetch data from a webpage directly, especially if the website doesn't provide an API. This is where **web**

scraping comes in. Web scraping is the process of extracting data from a website by parsing its HTML structure.

To scrape websites, we use the **BeautifulSoup** library in combination with the **requests** library.

2.1 Installing BeautifulSoup

First, install the required libraries:

bash

```bash
pip install beautifulsoup4 requests
```

BeautifulSoup helps parse HTML documents and extract data based on tags and attributes, like <div>, <a>, or <p>.

2.2 Basic Web Scraping with BeautifulSoup

Here's an example of how to scrape the headlines from a news website. Let's assume we're scraping the BBC website.

python

```python
import requests
from bs4 import BeautifulSoup

url = "https://www.bbc.com"
```

```
response = requests.get(url)

if response.status_code == 200:
    soup = BeautifulSoup(response.content,
'html.parser')

    # Find all the headlines
    headlines = soup.find_all('h3')

    for headline in headlines:
        print(headline.text)
else:
    print(f"Failed to retrieve data. Status code:
{response.status_code}")
```

In this code:

- We use `requests.get(url)` to fetch the HTML content of the webpage.
- We pass the content to BeautifulSoup (`BeautifulSoup(response.content, 'html.parser')`) to parse it.
- We use `soup.find_all('h3')` to find all `<h3>` tags, which typically represent headlines in many websites. You can adjust the tag based on the structure of the webpage you are scraping.

2.3 Extracting Specific Information

Web pages often contain various HTML tags. BeautifulSoup allows us to extract data based on tags, classes, or attributes. For example, if we want to extract all the links (<a> tags) from a page:

```python
url = "https://www.bbc.com"
response = requests.get(url)

if response.status_code == 200:
    soup = BeautifulSoup(response.content,
'html.parser')

    # Find all the links
    links = soup.find_all('a')

    for link in links:
        print(link.get('href'))  # Print the URL from
the href attribute
else:
    print(f"Failed to retrieve data. Status code:
{response.status_code}")
```

This code finds all <a> tags and extracts the href attribute, which contains the URLs of the links.

2.4 Handling Dynamic Content with Selenium

Many modern websites load content dynamically using JavaScript. BeautifulSoup works only with static HTML, meaning it won't be able to scrape content that is rendered by JavaScript after the page loads. For these types of websites, you can use **Selenium**, a browser automation tool that can render dynamic content.

To use Selenium for web scraping, you'll need to install the following:

```bash
bash
```

```bash
pip install selenium
```

You also need a **web driver**, such as ChromeDriver, to control a browser. Selenium will automate the browser to open the page and retrieve the dynamically loaded content.

Hands-On Project: Build a Program that Fetches the Latest News Headlines Using an API

Now, let's apply what we've learned by building a **news headline fetcher** that retrieves the latest headlines using an API. We'll use the

NewsAPI, a simple RESTful API for fetching live news articles from across the web.

Step 1: Get an API Key from NewsAPI

1. Visit NewsAPI.
2. Sign up for an account to get a free API key.

Once you have your API key, you can start making requests to fetch the latest news.

Step 2: Fetch Data from the API

Let's build a Python script that fetches the latest news headlines using the `requests` library.

```python
python

import requests

# Your NewsAPI key (replace with your own key)
api_key = 'your_api_key_here'

# NewsAPI endpoint for top headlines
url = f"https://newsapi.org/v2/top-
headlines?country=us&apiKey={api_key}"

response = requests.get(url)
```

```python
if response.status_code == 200:
    data = response.json()
    articles = data['articles']

    for article in articles:
        print(f"Headline: {article['title']}")
        print(f"Source: {article['source']['name']}")
        print(f"URL: {article['url']}")
        print("-" * 80)
else:
    print(f"Failed to fetch news:
{response.status_code}")
```

In this code:

- We make a GET request to the NewsAPI endpoint for the top headlines.
- We parse the JSON response and extract the articles.
- We print the title, source, and URL of each article.

Step 3: Testing the Application

Run the program, and it will print the latest news headlines, like this:

```makefile
Headline: 'Breaking News: Python Hits 20 Million
Downloads'
```

```
Source: BBC News
URL: https://www.bbc.com/news/technology-123456
-------------------------------------------------------
---------------------------
Headline: 'Stock Market Trends in 2022'
Source: CNN
URL: https://www.cnn.com/business/stocks-2022
-------------------------------------------------------
---------------------------
...
```

This program pulls live data from NewsAPI and displays it in a simple, readable format.

Step 4: Adding Error Handling and Logging

Now that we have the basic functionality working, let's improve the code by adding error handling and logging. This will ensure that the program can handle potential issues, like invalid API keys or connection problems.

```python
python

import logging
import requests

# Set up logging
logging.basicConfig(level=logging.INFO)
```

```python
api_key = 'your_api_key_here'
url = f"https://newsapi.org/v2/top-
headlines?country=us&apiKey={api_key}"

try:
    response = requests.get(url)
    response.raise_for_status()  # Raise an error for
bad HTTP status codes

    data = response.json()
    articles = data['articles']

    for article in articles:
        print(f"Headline: {article['title']}")
        print(f"Source: {article['source']['name']}")
        print(f"URL: {article['url']}")
        print("-" * 80)

except requests.exceptions.RequestException as e:
    logging.error(f"Error fetching news: {e}")
except KeyError as e:
    logging.error(f"Error parsing response: Missing
key {e}")
```

This updated version:

- Uses **logging** to record any errors.
- Handles **exceptions** that may occur during the API request or while parsing the response.

Takeaways: How to Pull and Manipulate Data from External Sources Using Python

By the end of this chapter, you should have learned how to:

1. **Work with APIs**: How to fetch data from external sources using APIs, parse JSON responses, and integrate external data into your Python applications.
2. **Web Scraping**: How to scrape data from websites using BeautifulSoup and how to handle dynamic content with tools like Selenium.
3. **Build Real-World Applications**: How to create a simple Python application that interacts with an API and fetches live news headlines.
4. **Error Handling and Logging**: How to add error handling and logging to your code, ensuring that your applications are robust and reliable.

APIs and web scraping are powerful tools for interacting with external data. By learning these techniques, you can enrich your applications with live data, automate data collection, and create highly interactive programs.

Chapter 14: Data Visualization with Matplotlib: Making Sense of Data

---

Overview: Learn How to Present Your Data Visually Using Python's Powerful Plotting Library

In today's data-driven world, visualizing your data is crucial to understanding trends, patterns, and insights that might otherwise be difficult to interpret. One of the most effective ways to communicate your findings is by using **data visualization**. Python, being one of the most widely used languages for data science, offers powerful tools for creating stunning visualizations, and one of the most popular libraries for this purpose is **Matplotlib**.

In this chapter, we'll learn how to:

- **Plot different types of graphs** (line graphs, bar charts, histograms, etc.) using **Matplotlib**.

- **Customize charts** to make them more informative and visually appealing.
- **Visualize datasets** in a way that highlights trends and patterns.
- Use data visualization to convey insights in real-world scenarios.

By the end of this chapter, you will be able to create your own visualizations and dashboards, such as a line graph that displays a business's sales over time. You will also gain a strong understanding of how to use **Matplotlib** to create various types of visualizations that can help you make better data-driven decisions.

Topics: Plotting Graphs, Customizing Charts, and Visualizing Datasets

1. Introduction to Matplotlib: A Powerful Plotting Library

Matplotlib is a comprehensive library for creating static, animated, and interactive visualizations in Python. It is built on top of **NumPy**, which makes it a great choice for working with numerical data. The library is highly customizable, allowing you to create a wide variety of charts and graphs.

The primary function of Matplotlib is to plot data in the form of various charts (e.g., line plots, bar charts, histograms), making it easier to visualize relationships between data points.

1.1 Installing Matplotlib

If you haven't already installed **Matplotlib**, you can do so using Python's package manager, **pip**:

bash

```
pip install matplotlib
```

Once installed, you can import it into your Python scripts using the following:

python

```
import matplotlib.pyplot as plt
```

1.2 Creating Basic Plots

The simplest plot you can create with Matplotlib is a **line plot**. Let's begin by plotting some basic data.

Example:

python

```
import matplotlib.pyplot as plt

# Data
x = [1, 2, 3, 4, 5]
y = [1, 4, 9, 16, 25]

# Create a line plot
plt.plot(x, y)

# Display the plot
plt.show()
```

In this example:

- `x` represents the x-axis data points.
- `y` represents the y-axis data points.
- `plt.plot(x, y)` creates a basic line graph.
- `plt.show()` displays the graph.

1.3 Adding Labels, Titles, and Gridlines

Matplotlib allows you to customize your plots by adding labels, titles, and gridlines.

python

```
plt.plot(x, y)
plt.title("Square Numbers")
plt.xlabel("X values")
```

```
plt.ylabel("Y values")
plt.grid(True)
plt.show()
```

In this enhanced plot:

- **plt.title("Square Numbers")** adds a title to the graph.
- **plt.xlabel("X values")** and **plt.ylabel("Y values")** label the x and y axes.
- **plt.grid(True)** adds gridlines to the plot for better readability.

2. Customizing Plots

One of the strengths of Matplotlib is its ability to customize every aspect of a plot. You can change colors, line styles, markers, and much more.

2.1 Customizing Line Styles and Colors

You can customize the line style and color using arguments in the `plt.plot()` function.

Example:

```python
python
```

```
plt.plot(x, y, color="green", linestyle="--",
marker="o")
plt.title("Customized Line Plot")
plt.xlabel("X values")
plt.ylabel("Y values")
plt.grid(True)
plt.show()
```

In this example:

- **color="green"** sets the line color to green.
- **linestyle="--"** sets the line to a dashed style.
- **marker="o"** adds circular markers at each data point.

2.2 Adding Legends

Legends help identify different data series on a plot. You can add a legend to your plot using the `label` parameter.

Example:

python

```
plt.plot(x, y, label="Square Numbers", color="blue")
plt.title("Plot with Legend")
plt.xlabel("X values")
plt.ylabel("Y values")
plt.legend()
plt.grid(True)
```

```
plt.show()
```

The `plt.legend()` function places a legend on the plot, which refers to the label of the data series.

3. Plotting Different Types of Graphs

Matplotlib supports various types of graphs to visualize data, including line plots, bar charts, histograms, and scatter plots. Let's explore a few of them.

3.1 Bar Chart

A **bar chart** is useful for comparing quantities across different categories. Here's how to create one:

Example:

python

```python
categories = ['A', 'B', 'C', 'D']
values = [3, 7, 5, 2]

plt.bar(categories, values, color='purple')
plt.title("Bar Chart Example")
plt.xlabel("Categories")
plt.ylabel("Values")
plt.show()
```

In this example:

- `categories` represents the different categories (A, B, C, D).
- `values` represents the values associated with each category.
- `plt.bar(categories, values)` creates the bar chart.

3.2 Histogram

A **histogram** is used to visualize the distribution of a dataset. Here's how to plot one:

Example:

```python
import numpy as np

data = np.random.randn(1000)   # Generate random data

plt.hist(data, bins=30, color='skyblue',
edgecolor='black')
plt.title("Histogram Example")
plt.xlabel("Value")
plt.ylabel("Frequency")
plt.show()
```

In this example:

- `np.random.randn(1000)` generates 1000 random numbers from a normal distribution.
- `plt.hist(data, bins=30)` creates a histogram with 30 bins.

3.3 Scatter Plot

A **scatter plot** is used to display the relationship between two continuous variables. Let's create a scatter plot:

Example:

python

```
x = np.random.rand(50)
y = np.random.rand(50)

plt.scatter(x, y, color='red')
plt.title("Scatter Plot Example")
plt.xlabel("X values")
plt.ylabel("Y values")
plt.show()
```

In this example:

- `np.random.rand(50)` generates 50 random data points for both x and y.
- `plt.scatter(x, y)` creates a scatter plot with red points.

4. Visualizing Datasets

Once you've learned how to create basic plots, the next step is to visualize real datasets. In this section, we'll explore how to load datasets and visualize them using Matplotlib.

4.1 Using Pandas for Data Manipulation

Pandas is a popular library for data manipulation in Python. It provides data structures like **DataFrame** and **Series** to handle and process datasets. We'll use Pandas to load a dataset and then visualize it using Matplotlib.

Install Pandas with:

bash

```
pip install pandas
```

Example: Visualizing sales data over time.

python

```
import pandas as pd

# Sample data
data = {'Date': ['2021-01-01', '2021-01-02', '2021-
01-03', '2021-01-04', '2021-01-05'],
```

```
       'Sales': [100, 150, 200, 180, 220]}

# Create a DataFrame
df = pd.DataFrame(data)

# Convert the Date column to datetime
df['Date'] = pd.to_datetime(df['Date'])

# Plot the data
plt.plot(df['Date'], df['Sales'], color='green',
marker='o', label='Sales')
plt.title("Sales Trend Over Time")
plt.xlabel("Date")
plt.ylabel("Sales")
plt.xticks(rotation=45)   # Rotate the x-axis labels
for better readability
plt.grid(True)
plt.legend()
plt.show()
```

In this example:

- We created a **DataFrame** using Pandas and visualized it using Matplotlib.
- The `plt.xticks(rotation=45)` line rotates the x-axis labels to make them more readable.

4.2 Plotting Multiple Datasets

You may want to plot multiple datasets on the same chart for comparison. Matplotlib allows you to easily overlay multiple plots.

Example:

python

```
# Sample data
sales = [100, 150, 200, 180, 220]
expenses = [80, 120, 160, 140, 180]

plt.plot(df['Date'], sales, label="Sales",
color="blue", marker="o")
plt.plot(df['Date'], expenses, label="Expenses",
color="red", marker="x")
plt.title("Sales vs Expenses")
plt.xlabel("Date")
plt.ylabel("Amount")
plt.legend()
plt.grid(True)
plt.show()
```

In this case, we are plotting both **Sales** and **Expenses** on the same graph for comparison.

5. Building a Dashboard: Displaying Data Trends

Now, let's take everything we've learned and create a simple **dashboard** that displays trends, such as a line graph for business sales over time. This is a more advanced visualization that incorporates multiple components into one cohesive layout.

5.1 Organizing Multiple Plots

We can display multiple charts in a single window using `subplot()`. This function allows us to specify a grid layout for multiple plots.

Example:

python

```
fig, (ax1, ax2) = plt.subplots(1, 2, figsize=(12, 6))

# Plotting sales on ax1
ax1.plot(df['Date'], df['Sales'], color='green',
marker='o')
ax1.set_title("Sales Trend")
ax1.set_xlabel("Date")
ax1.set_ylabel("Sales")

# Plotting expenses on ax2
ax2.plot(df['Date'], expenses, color='red',
marker='x')
```

```
ax2.set_title("Expenses Trend")
ax2.set_xlabel("Date")
ax2.set_ylabel("Expenses")

plt.tight_layout()  # Adjusts spacing between plots
plt.show()
```

In this example:

- `plt.subplots(1, 2)` creates a 1x2 grid of subplots, allowing us to display two charts side by side.
- `ax1` and `ax2` are the individual axes (subplots) where we plot the data.

5.2 Interactive Dashboards with Plotly

For more complex dashboards, you can use **Plotly,** a Python library that allows you to create interactive plots. Unlike Matplotlib, Plotly supports interactive features like zooming, hovering, and clicking.

To get started with Plotly:

```bash
bash
```

```
pip install plotly
```

You can create interactive visualizations with Plotly, which are especially useful for web-based dashboards.

Takeaways: How to Visualize Data Effectively Using Matplotlib

By the end of this chapter, you should have learned:

1. **How to Use Matplotlib**: You now understand the basics of using Matplotlib to create various types of graphs, including line plots, bar charts, histograms, and scatter plots.
2. **How to Customize Plots**: You can enhance the clarity of your charts by customizing their appearance—adding labels, titles, legends, and gridlines.
3. **How to Work with Datasets**: Using Pandas alongside Matplotlib, you can load datasets and visualize trends, comparing multiple data series on the same graph.
4. **How to Build Dashboards**: You have learned how to organize multiple plots into a cohesive layout, which is a basic form of a dashboard for data analysis.

Data visualization is a crucial skill for any data scientist or developer. By learning to create effective and visually appealing charts, you can communicate insights clearly and make data-driven decisions.

Chapter 15: Final Project: Creating Your First Python Application

Overview: The Culmination of Everything You've Learned

At this point, you've gained a solid understanding of Python's core concepts, from working with basic syntax and data types to diving into object-oriented programming, APIs, data visualization, and even building microservices. This chapter marks the culmination of everything you've learned so far.

In this chapter, we'll take a step-by-step approach to planning, designing, and building a fully functional Python application. Whether you're interested in tracking your personal finances, creating a weather dashboard, or building another project, this chapter will provide you with a comprehensive guide to constructing a complete app from scratch.

The goal of this chapter is to:

- **Put your knowledge to work** by applying it to a real-world project.
- **Structure a large project** to ensure that it is modular, maintainable, and scalable.
- **Implement practical features** using the tools and libraries you've learned, such as **APIs, file handling, OOP**, and **visualization**.

By the end of this chapter, you'll not only have a working Python application, but you'll also have the experience of putting together a larger project that can serve as a valuable portfolio piece.

Topics: Planning, Designing, and Building a Full Application from Scratch

1. Planning Your Application

Before you start writing code, it's crucial to **plan** your application. Good planning sets the foundation for a smooth development process and ensures that your app is well-structured, functional, and easy to maintain.

1.1 Defining the Purpose of the Application

The first step in planning your project is to define its **purpose**. Ask yourself:

- What problem does this application solve?
- Who will use the application?
- What are the key features and functionalities of the app?

For example, if you're building a **personal finance tracker**, your app will help users track their expenses, income, and budget. Key features might include:

- Adding and categorizing expenses.
- Viewing monthly reports.
- Setting budget limits and tracking progress.
- Generating charts for data visualization.

For a **weather dashboard**, your app will fetch real-time weather data and display it in a user-friendly format. Key features could include:

- Displaying the current weather for a given location.
- Showing a 7-day weather forecast.
- Adding custom locations to track multiple cities.
- Visualizing temperature and weather trends using graphs.

1.2 Designing the Application's Structure

Once you've defined the purpose, it's time to **design** the application's structure. Think of this as creating a blueprint for your app. Here are the key design steps:

- **Break the application into components**: Think about the different features your app will have and how they will be organized. For example, in a finance tracker, components might include:
    - A **data entry** interface to input expenses and income.
    - A **reporting** system to generate monthly or yearly financial summaries.
    - A **budget tracking** system to alert users when they exceed their budget.
- **Identify the data flow**: Where will your app get its data from? Will it be stored locally in files or in a database? If it's an API-based app, what external data sources will you use (such as a weather API or a financial data API)?
- **Decide on the technology stack**: Choose the libraries and tools that are most suited for your app. For example:
    - **APIs** for fetching live data (e.g., OpenWeather for weather data).
    - **Matplotlib** for visualizations (e.g., graphs for financial data).

o **Tkinter** for creating a basic graphical user interface (GUI), or **Flask** if you prefer a web app.

1.3 Structuring the Code

Once you know what features you need and how the data will flow, it's time to think about the **structure** of your code. When building a larger project, it's important to organize your code so it's maintainable, scalable, and easy to navigate.

Here are some best practices for structuring your Python project:

- **Use functions and classes** to organize the logic.
- **Create separate files for different components** of the application (e.g., one for data handling, one for the user interface, one for the API interaction).
- **Write tests** for important functions to ensure the app behaves as expected.

For example, if you're building a weather dashboard, you could structure the code like this:

- **weather_api.py**: Handles the interaction with the weather API.
- **data_processing.py**: Processes and formats the fetched weather data.

- **visualization.py**: Generates graphs to display the weather trends.
- **main.py**: The entry point of the application that integrates everything.

---

2. Designing the User Interface (UI)

The next step in planning is to think about how the user will interact with your application. The user interface (UI) is the bridge between your code and the user, so it's important to make it intuitive and easy to navigate.

2.1 User Interface for a Console-Based App

If you're building a console-based app (no GUI), the UI will consist of text prompts and responses in the terminal. In this case, you'll want to design a clear, user-friendly way for the user to input data and view results.

For a **personal finance tracker**, the UI could look something like this:

- Prompt for entering expenses, income, and setting budgets.
- Display a summary of the user's finances (e.g., total expenses, remaining budget, monthly report).

- Use **menus** to navigate between different sections of the app (e.g., enter data, view reports, generate graphs).

2.2 User Interface for a Graphical App

For a **graphical user interface (GUI)**, you might use a library like **Tkinter**, which is built into Python, or **PyQt** or **Kivy** for more advanced interfaces. A weather dashboard, for example, could have the following:

- A search bar for entering the city name.
- A display area showing the current weather.
- A graph showing temperature trends over the next few days.
- Buttons to add favorite cities.

Hands-On Project: Build a Fully Functional Python App

Let's take the planning and design steps and apply them to build a simple **personal finance tracker**. This project will incorporate user input, file handling, and basic data visualization.

Step 1: Setting Up the Project

First, let's outline the basic functionality of the personal finance tracker:

- **Add Income/Expense**: The app will allow users to add their income and expenses.
- **View Summary**: The app will display a summary of total income, total expenses, and remaining budget.
- **Set Budget**: Users can set a budget, and the app will track their spending.

Step 2: Create the Task and Budget Classes

Using **Object-Oriented Programming (OOP)**, we'll create classes to represent the **Task** (representing income or expense) and **Budget** (to track the budget).

python

```python
class Task:
    def __init__(self, description, amount, category, date):
        self.description = description
        self.amount = amount
        self.category = category
        self.date = date
```

```python
    def __str__(self):
        return f"{self.description}: {self.amount} on
{self.date}"

class Budget:
    def __init__(self, total_budget):
        self.total_budget = total_budget
        self.balance = total_budget
        self.transactions = []

    def add_transaction(self, task):
        self.transactions.append(task)
        self.balance -= task.amount

    def get_summary(self):
        total_income = sum([t.amount for t in
self.transactions if t.amount > 0])
        total_expenses = sum([t.amount for t in
self.transactions if t.amount < 0])
        return {
            "total_income": total_income,
            "total_expenses": total_expenses,
            "balance": self.balance
        }
```

The Task class represents an individual transaction (income or expense), while the Budget class tracks the total budget and calculates the balance after each transaction.

Step 3: Saving Data to a File

We'll use file handling to save the user's income and expense data.
This ensures that the data persists between app sessions.

python

```python
import json

def save_data(budget, filename="budget_data.json"):
    with open(filename, 'w') as file:
        data = {
            "total_budget": budget.total_budget,
            "transactions": [{"description":
t.description, "amount": t.amount, "category":
t.category, "date": t.date} for t in
budget.transactions]
        }
        json.dump(data, file)

def load_data(filename="budget_data.json"):
    try:
        with open(filename, 'r') as file:
            data = json.load(file)
            budget = Budget(data["total_budget"])
            for transaction in data["transactions"]:
                task =
Task(transaction["description"],
```

```
transaction["amount"], transaction["category"],
transaction["date"])
                budget.add_transaction(task)
            return budget
    except FileNotFoundError:
        return Budget(0)  # Start with zero budget if
no data exists
```

This function saves the budget and transaction data to a JSON file and loads it back when the app starts.

Step 4: Creating the User Interface

Now, let's create a simple text-based user interface for the personal finance tracker.

python

```python
def display_menu():
    print("Personal Finance Tracker")
    print("1. Add Income")
    print("2. Add Expense")
    print("3. View Summary")
    print("4. Save and Exit")

def add_transaction_prompt(budget, transaction_type):
    description = input("Enter description: ")
    amount = float(input("Enter amount: "))
    category = input("Enter category: ")
```

```python
    date = input("Enter date (YYYY-MM-DD): ")

    task = Task(description, amount, category, date)
    if transaction_type == 'income':
        budget.add_transaction(task)
    elif transaction_type == 'expense':
        task.amount = -task.amount  # Make the amount
negative for expenses
        budget.add_transaction(task)


def main():
    budget = load_data()

    while True:
        display_menu()
        choice = input("Choose an option: ")

        if choice == "1":
            add_transaction_prompt(budget, 'income')
        elif choice == "2":
            add_transaction_prompt(budget, 'expense')
        elif choice == "3":
            summary = budget.get_summary()
            print(f"Total Income:
{summary['total_income']}")
            print(f"Total Expenses:
{summary['total_expenses']}")
            print(f"Remaining Balance:
{summary['balance']}")
```

```
elif choice == "4":
    save_data(budget)
    print("Data saved. Goodbye!")
    break
else:
    print("Invalid choice. Please try
again.")


# Run the application
main()
```

Step 5: Running the Application

Once the code is in place, you can run the program and:

- Add income or expense transactions.
- View a summary of your finances.
- Save your data to a file and load it again when you start the application.

Step 6: Enhancing the App (Optional)

You can extend this app by:

- Adding more detailed categories (e.g., "Food", "Entertainment").
- Implementing **data visualization** using **Matplotlib** to visualize monthly spending and income.

- Adding **graphical user interface (GUI)** elements with **Tkinter** or **PyQt** to make the app more user-friendly.

Takeaways: How to Structure a Large Project and Put Your Knowledge to Work

By the end of this chapter, you should have learned how to:

1. **Plan and Design**: You learned how to structure a project by defining the problem, breaking it into components, and planning the overall design.
2. **Build a Python Application**: You learned how to implement features using Python and organize them in a structured way.
3. **Use OOP**: You applied Object-Oriented Programming principles to design classes and methods for a well-structured application.
4. **Implement File Handling**: You learned how to use file handling to save and load data.
5. **Create a Simple Console Application**: You built a simple command-line interface that allows users to interact with your application.

This chapter demonstrates how to integrate the various Python concepts you've learned into a single, cohesive project. By building your first Python application, you've taken a major step toward becoming a proficient Python developer. As you continue developing and enhancing this application or start new projects, you'll be able to apply these skills to solve real-world problems.

Conclusion: Next Steps in Your Python Journey

Recap of Everything Covered in the Book

As we reach the end of this guide, let's take a moment to recap everything you've learned throughout your Python journey. By now, you should have a solid foundation in Python programming and be comfortable with key concepts and practical applications. This book has taken you through a comprehensive learning experience, covering everything from basic syntax to advanced programming concepts, all of which have prepared you to build functional and meaningful applications.

Here's a summary of the key topics we've explored:

1. **Introduction to Python**:
    - You began with the essentials of Python, including setting up your development environment and understanding the basic syntax.
    - You learned how to work with variables, data types, and operators to perform basic calculations.

2. **Control Flow and Functions**:
   - You explored conditionals (if, elif, else) and loops (for, while) to control the flow of your programs.
   - Functions were introduced as a way to organize code, allowing for code reuse and better structure.

3. **Object-Oriented Programming (OOP)**:
   - You dove into the world of OOP, where you learned how to create classes and objects, as well as how to use attributes and methods.
   - You explored inheritance and polymorphism to make your code more reusable and scalable.

4. **Working with External Libraries**:
   - You gained an understanding of how to expand Python's capabilities by working with third-party libraries like `requests` and `beautifulsoup`.
   - You learned how to fetch live data from APIs and scrape web content, opening up new possibilities for building applications that interact with external sources.

5. **Data Visualization with Matplotlib**:
   - You learned how to visualize data using Matplotlib, one of Python's most powerful libraries for creating charts and graphs.

- o   You explored various types of charts like line graphs, bar charts, and scatter plots, and learned how to customize them to make the data easier to interpret.

6. **Building Microservices:**
   - o   You delved into the concept of microservices, breaking down large applications into smaller, more manageable services.
   - o   You learned how to build microservices with Python using Flask, and how to enable communication between these services via APIs.

7. **Final Project:**
   - o   You applied everything you learned by building a fully functional Python application, such as a **personal finance tracker** or a **weather dashboard**.
   - o   Through this project, you structured your code, handled data, and built a user interface, bringing together the concepts you learned throughout the book.

You've not only built an understanding of core Python concepts but also put them into practice by developing real-world applications. This process of creating working software, troubleshooting problems, and refining your projects is crucial in mastering Python.

Encouragement to Continue Practicing and Exploring More Advanced Concepts

While you've learned a lot in this book, this is just the beginning of your Python journey. Python is a vast language with an ever-growing ecosystem of tools, frameworks, and libraries, and there is always more to learn. The key to becoming proficient in Python—or in any programming language—is consistent practice and exploration.

Here are some important points to keep in mind as you continue your Python journey:

1. Keep Coding and Building Projects

The best way to solidify what you've learned is by building projects. The more you code, the more you'll understand the nuances of Python. Try to tackle different types of projects to challenge yourself and explore new aspects of the language.

- **Web Development**: Learn how to build web applications using **Flask** or **Django**, two popular Python frameworks.
- **Data Science**: Explore data science libraries like **Pandas, NumPy, SciPy**, and **Scikit-learn** for working with data, performing statistical analysis, and building machine learning models.

- **Game Development**: Explore **Pygame** to build simple games. This is a fun way to apply your knowledge of Python and enhance your skills.
- **Automation**: Start automating tasks in your personal or professional life. Use Python to scrape data from websites, automate workflows, or analyze large datasets.

2. Explore Advanced Python Topics

As you continue your learning, consider diving into more advanced Python concepts that will make you a more versatile programmer.

- **Decorators and Generators**: Learn how to use decorators to modify the behavior of functions and generators to handle large datasets efficiently.
- **Concurrency and Parallelism**: Understand the basics of multi-threading and multi-processing to write faster, more efficient code.
- **Design Patterns**: Learn common design patterns, which provide reusable solutions to common problems encountered in software design.
- **Unit Testing**: Familiarize yourself with unit testing in Python using **unittest** or **pytest**. This will help you write more reliable and maintainable code.

- **Database Integration**: Learn how to connect your Python applications to databases, whether it's **SQL** (PostgreSQL, MySQL) or **NoSQL** (MongoDB), to store and manage data.

3. Contribute to Open Source Projects

One of the best ways to learn is by collaborating with other developers. Contributing to open-source Python projects is a great way to gain practical experience and improve your coding skills. You can find open-source Python projects on platforms like **GitHub** and contribute to them by fixing bugs, adding new features, or improving documentation.

Contributing to open source not only strengthens your coding abilities but also gives you the chance to interact with experienced developers, learn best practices, and build your reputation within the developer community.

4. Learn Additional Tools and Frameworks

Beyond the core Python language, there are a number of additional tools and frameworks that you can learn to further enhance your programming skills. Some of these include:

- **Docker**: Learn how to containerize your Python applications with Docker to make them portable and easy to deploy.

- **Celery**: For handling asynchronous tasks in Python applications, particularly useful for web applications that require background processing.
- **Flask & Django**: Web development frameworks that allow you to build and deploy web applications quickly.
- **TensorFlow** or **PyTorch**: Libraries for building machine learning and deep learning models.
- **Pytest**: A testing framework that allows you to write unit tests for your Python code.

These tools will expand your toolkit and allow you to tackle a broader range of development challenges.

Resources for Further Learning and Getting Involved in the Python Community

As you continue your Python journey, here are some helpful resources and communities to guide you in learning more and staying up-to-date with the latest developments in Python:

1. Official Documentation

The official **Python documentation** is an invaluable resource. It provides detailed explanations of Python's standard library, language features, and best practices.

- **Python Docs**: https://docs.python.org

2. Online Learning Platforms

There are many excellent platforms that offer Python tutorials, courses, and certification programs. These resources are great for structured learning and diving deeper into specific topics.

- **Codecademy**: Offers interactive courses on Python and many other programming languages.
- **Coursera**: Provides courses from top universities and companies, including courses focused on Python for data science, web development, and machine learning.
- **edX**: Offers online Python courses, including free courses from universities like MIT and Harvard.
- **Real Python**: An excellent resource for both beginner and advanced Python tutorials and guides.

3. Python Books for Advanced Learners

If you prefer learning from books, there are many great books that dive deeper into Python and its applications. Some recommendations include:

- **"Fluent Python"** by Luciano Ramalho (for advanced Python concepts).
- **"Python Crash Course"** by Eric Matthes (a hands-on introduction to Python).
- **"Python Data Science Handbook"** by Jake VanderPlas (focused on Python for data science).

4. Python Communities

The Python community is large, welcoming, and supportive. Engaging with other Python developers is a great way to learn, get help with problems, and contribute to the community.

- **Stack Overflow**: A massive community of developers where you can ask and answer programming questions.
- **Reddit (r/learnpython)**: A community of Python learners who share resources, projects, and advice.
- **Python Discord**: A real-time community for Python developers to chat, share projects, and get help.

- **PyCon**: The annual Python conference, which offers great networking opportunities and learning sessions.

5. Participating in Python Meetups and Conferences

Attending Python meetups or conferences is a great way to connect with fellow Python enthusiasts and learn from experts. PyCon, for example, is one of the biggest Python conferences in the world and hosts talks, tutorials, and workshops for developers of all skill levels.

You can find local meetups and events through websites like:

- **Meetup.com**: Search for Python-related meetups near you.
- **PyCon**: Learn more about PyCon and other Python conferences at https://www.pycon.org.

6. Contributing to Open Source

Open-source contributions allow you to work with other developers, practice real-world coding, and give back to the community. GitHub is the primary platform for open-source projects, and you can find Python projects of all sizes that need contributors. Some repositories offer beginner-friendly issues to help newcomers get started.

To start contributing:

- Browse projects on **GitHub:** https://github.com
- Look for **beginner issues:** Many repositories tag beginner-friendly issues as `good first issue`.

Final Words: Stay Curious and Keep Growing

Now that you've completed this book, you've laid the foundation for becoming a proficient Python developer. But the journey doesn't stop here. Python is an incredibly versatile language with a huge ecosystem of tools and libraries to explore. Whether you're interested in web development, data science, machine learning, game development, or automation, Python has something for you.

As you continue to learn, don't hesitate to take on more challenging projects, contribute to open-source software, and engage with the global Python community. The more you practice and build, the more confident and proficient you'll become.

Remember: **Programming is a journey, not a destination.** Every new concept you learn and every project you build will bring you closer to mastering Python and becoming a successful developer.

Keep experimenting, stay curious, and continue coding!

Happy coding!